The poems and stories in this anthology are true tales; however, some names have been changed to protect people's privacy.

The acknowledgements pages constitute a continuation of the copyright page.

ISBN 979-8-9904733-4-8
Open edition

Design and typeset by chuck kuan
Proofreading by Kelly Jean Fitzsimmons
Cover and interior art by A King McCarty

Published by Poets of Queens Press
poetsofqueens.com

PROM QUEENS:

CELEBRATING PROM POEMS & STORIES BY QUEENS WRITERS

edited by Kelly Jean Fitzsimmons, Pichchenda Bao, & Tim Lindner

Poets of Queens and No, YOU Tell It!
New York, 2026

Poets of Queens and No, YOU Tell It! are proud to partner to publish this anthology.

POETS OF QUEENS creates a community for poetry in Queens and beyond. The reading series creates a connection between a diverse group of poets and an audience. Poets of Queens publishes individual collections and anthologies to help poets connect to their community through their work.

NO, YOU TELL IT! storytellers work together to develop true tales on the page, then swap stories to embody their story partner's culture, identity, and life experience on stage.

The stories by Tim Lindner, Jane Frances, Vegas K Jarrow, and Ricki Richards were developed and performed as part of a special No, YOU Tell It! "Prom Queens" show at Grove 34 in Astoria on September 17, 2025.

Learn more at noyoutellit.com and listen to live story swaps from the "Prom Queens" show and more on the No, YOU Tell It! podcast, available on all major platforms.

Visit poetsofqueens.com to learn more about the reading series and how to submit.

This anthology is dedicated to Olena Jennings, Zach Rothman-Hicks, and A King McCarty, fabulous friends and fantastic collaborators for the series of *Prom Queens: Prom Story and Portrait Trading Workshops* that helped inspire these prom poems and stories.

Special thanks to No, YOU Tell It! creative team members Pichchenda Bao, Tim Lindner, and Erika Iverson for the emotional and editorial support from the first word to the final edit.

Sending love to all who contributed to these beautiful pages and please share your prom story!

Table of Contents

Foreword: Part 1

Kelly Jean Fitzsimmons

Prom originates from the pagan ritual celebrating the deity Promnestra, an ancient Celtic goddess representing frivolity, fortune, and female rivalry. On the first day of spring, all the neighboring tribes would send their virginal, of-age daughters to compete in a grueling tournament of Sean-nós dancing. Extremely distinctive by its footwork, which stays parallel and primarily touches the ground, Sean-nós dancers donned bright robes, tightly wrapped at the waist and bodice, allowing their hips and upper arms to sway in more improvisational movements.

Months of preparation went into making the ritual Promnestra dress because, as legend has it, if two competitors arrived wearing the same frock, they had no choice but to fight to the death. The remaining girls danced individually, often for days, passing out from fatigue until a sole virgin was left standing. This fortunate young woman would then be crowned as the Promnestra Queen and paired with a king. Escorting her to the throne of fertility, the Promnestra King poured the blood from a freshly sacrificed sow over the young woman's head before whisking his queen off to a local motel room he'd booked for the night.

Of course, none of this is true. Prom is painted as the pinnacle of high school, often outshining graduation. When I started researching prom for my memoir *After After Prom*, which examines prom as an American rite of passage interwoven with my personal prom story, I'd imagined its origin story to be steeped in ancient mythos. Sadly, though, there is no goddess Promnestra or traditional battle royale over wearing the same dress.

So, why is prom such a big deal?

Once upon a time, the idea of graduating high school without going to prom was the worst fate I could imagine. The promise of prom night made me believe that if I could transform myself into the kind of girl whom "The Boy" I secretly loved would ask to prom, then I was guaranteed a happy ending.

As the 30th anniversary of my prom night approached, I decided it wasn't just my prom story that needed to be told.

Sharing stories about going or not going to prom allows us to find commonalities within each other's unique cultures and identities. In 2025, I received a Queens Art Fund (QAF): New Work Grant from the New York Foundation for the Arts in support of my project pairing generative writing workshops with a call for submissions for an anthology of real people's prom stories instead of the prom myth polished by pop culture. My aim for the series of generative workshops that I co-facilitated with Zach Rothman-Hicks (Gabbing with Gays) was to curate a collection that would help people, including future prom-goers, celebrate each other's prom stories instead of feeling pressured to live up to what we've been told prom is supposed to look like.

My nonfiction series No, YOU Tell It! (noyoutellit.com) brings storytellers together to trade tales, speak each other's words, and empower voices on the page and stage. Building off the QAF grant, No, YOU Tell It! was thrilled to partner with Olena Jennings and Poets of Queens to curate this *Prom Queens* (get it?) anthology celebrating prom poems and stories from Queens writers. What better place to give voice to a diverse range of prom stories than The World's Borough!

The real origins of prom stem from its name. Prom is short for *promenade*, a French word meaning "a leisurely walk." This slow walk also refers to the parade of guests, often in pairs, which acts as an opening ceremony for a cotillion or debutante ball. Inspired by No, YOU Tell It!'s practice of creating story partners who help each other share the stories that need to be told, the anthology is arranged as a poetry and prose promenade of paired *Prom Queens* contributors. Each promenade pair is introduced by an illustration capturing their combined spirit by Queens artist and contributor A King McCarty, whose "Zombie Prom Queen" poem/song originated in one of the generative workshops.

Our book events will feature poetry and prose promenade pairs trading prom tales and reading each other's words aloud. Likewise, attendees will be encouraged to share their prom story by filling in the blanks of a series of *PROMpts* that were part of our 2025 No, YOU Tell It! "Prom Queens" show at Grove 34 in Astoria, Queens.

However you've found your way to this anthology, you are welcome to fill out one of the following *PROMpts* to share your story:

My prom: looked ________________, smelled ________________, sounded ________________, felt ________________, and tasted ________________.

Instead of going to prom, I ________________ and it was ____.

Something I don't want to remember about prom night is ____.

A significant person in my prom story is ________________ because ____.

When I go to prom, I know that the night will be filled with __________ because I am ____.

Prom is a shortened version of promenade, but the original intent was to expand access beyond high society to create a ball for all where any teenager could dance the night away. Prom goes wrong when people feel pressured to conform to one version of how prom night should go and how its goers should look—the prom story decreed to be the *right* one.

Prom night's true power comes from the community created through shared experiences. Whether you had a magical, meh, or no prom, I invite you to attend our ball for all and parade alongside our *Prom Queens* poetry and prose promenade. Add your prom story, or what you did instead, by sending your completed *PROMpt* to noyoutellit@gmail.com.

We will share selected ones anonymously on our website and through social media to continue our celebration of prom poems and stories, Queens writers, and you.

Foreword: Part 2

Zach Rothman-Hicks

Prom is a unifying theme, whether prom was the worst night of our lives, the best, or somewhere in between. As a shy, closeted gay male growing up in the '90s, going to prom wasn't on my radar. That was something which cool, popular, normal kids did, and I didn't belong in any of those categories. There weren't any gay kids on the TGIF sitcoms playing on ABC in the '90s who went to prom. However, during senior year, I unexpectedly found my tribe of misfits, and we all decided to go to prom together. Even though I didn't have a date per se, it felt great to be part of a friend group and do something that cool, normal kids also did. Prom was an important milestone in my social development.

Many would argue that it's easier to openly identify as LGBTQIA+ in 2026 than it was 30 years ago, but certain rites of passage, such as prom, can still be quite challenging. The world reminds us daily that homophobia and transphobia, among other dangers, are not far below the surface. In April 2020, I co-founded Gabbing with Gays, which is an interdisciplinary oral history and community-building project. Gabbing with Gays carves out an emotionally intimate, liminal space for those in the LGBTQIA+ community and their allies. Being present for the sharing of emotionally intimate stories reminded me of the power of giving LGBTQIA+ people the tools to express their authentic selves and share meaningful experiences.

Many LGBTQIA+ people have had to repress parts of their identity in order to maintain their physical and emotional safety and security. Some of the poems and stories in this anthology speak to the highs, lows, excitement, awkwardness, and everything in between that go into being a queer person in a historically straight setting. Giving voice to the queer prom experience will help give others the courage to come forward and share their stories. They will see that they do not have to let fear define them because they are not alone.

From May through July 2025, I had the pleasure of collaborating with Kelly Jean Fitzsimmons (No, YOU Tell It!) and Olena Jennings (Poets of Queens) on a series of *Prom Queens: Prom Story and Portrait Trading Workshops* around Queens. During these free, generative workshops that I co-facilitated with Kelly Jean, participants were invited to share their prom stories through a series of written and visual prompts. The first half featured generative writing prompts to help participants brainstorm their prom stories—or what they did instead. Then we paired people up as story partners, who interviewed each other to learn more. In the second half, the story partners traced each other's faces on transparency paper and incorporated what they heard in their prom stories to create a symbolic, composite portrait of their partner. Finally, participants shared the portraits they made and the prom stories behind them. The *Prom Queens* workshops were paired with a call for submissions for the anthology, and much of what you are about to read started with those prom story and portrait swaps.

Having co-facilitated the *Prom Queens* workshops and heard so many powerful prom stories shared verbally, it is exciting to see them come to fruition as poems and stories on the page. Jane Frances shared one story during our first *Prom Queens* workshop and later as a storyteller for the No, YOU Tell It! "Prom Queens" show that resonated with me. She reflected on the pressure faced on multiple fronts when approaching prom: from the social pressure to attend prom, to her conservative Filipino mother's expectations for what she should wear, to the general discomfort of being closeted in a very heterosexual environment.

As a gay man, I can relate to the part of Jane's story where she expresses the pressure of having to stifle oneself in order to fit into a heterosexual rite of passage. Although I deeply appreciated having a group of friends to go to my prom with, I, too, experienced it from the closet. This line resonated with the audience and me when Jane's "A Prom Story" was performed on stage by her story partner: "but I just felt awkward; it felt strange to be in the crowd, moving around, trying to imitate and follow along with what he was doing, moving around in this dress I didn't want to be in." I also stifled a deep part of myself in order to be safe and fit in at prom, which has been the experience of many LGBTQIA+ people.

Lakshmi Gandhi's story originated at that same *Prom Queens* workshop and serves as a guidebook to prom that artfully explores the highs, lows, and everything in between, while also addressing the added challenges faced by second-generation immigrants. Reading about the social and economic pressures of prom through the lens of a child of immigrants further highlights the toxicity and deep challenges present in many people's prom experience. Lakshmi's puzzlement about prom customs parallels the confusion people outside the U.S. express when they first hear about Black Friday. Americans have become accustomed to traditions such as prom and Black Friday, and seeing them through a fresh set of eyes is informative, as it reminds us that parts of these traditions are problematic.

The inclusion of both the LGBTQIA+ perspective and the diverse Queens authors' experiences in this anthology ensures full representation of prom experiences. Hearing prom stories from such a diverse range of people, both spoken and written, is a reminder of the incredible power that all stories have for making us better human beings.

"Everything I ever dreamed."

"only us."

After a Friend in High School Reads My Palm and Tells Me There's a Break in My Lifeline

Pichchenda Bao

I look back and see
a whole-hearted girl
who would do anything
to love, for love was
the one thing
she thought she
was no good for
and she was
hard-headed and
determined to prove
herself wrong.
See her getting all
dolled up for prom.
Hair and makeup and manicure.
A proper ball gown.
Her date is handsome
and chaste, like Ken.

Let me say, it was
perfect. Everything
I ever dreamed.
And if I looked,
I might still find
the desiccated corsage
kept safe in a keepsafe box
faintly scented with decay.

Prom with Rain

Tim Lindner

"Hi, Timmy," a young, chubby girl named Ashley with frizzy hair and a gap in her teeth said, approaching me cautiously.

"Hey, Ashley," I said, holding my left wrist with my right hand across my tummy. My buzzed haircut was starting to grow out, revealing cowlicks in the front and back.

"The rash is bad this year, huh?"

She was talking about my poison ivy. Every year in elementary school, I awoke with a rash all over my body. In the early years, I stayed home, but once we discovered it wasn't contagious, my parents sent me to school.

"I'm trying not to scratch it," I tensed, adjusting my glasses, calamine lotion smearing, "and Jaimie and her stupid friends keep calling me Poison Ivy Boy."

"What-ever, it'll be gone in a few days," sympathized Ashley, "I'll never be as pretty as them."

"Shut up!"

It was the '90s, and bullying was still allowed. Over the years, though, we evolved, appearing more normal, especially once we started mixing schools in middle and high school. I lost the glasses and some people even thought I was cute! I was smart, just different enough, and had friends across different cliques, even if I couldn't see them without my glasses.

Ashley had her Laney Boggs in *She's All That* moment in tenth grade. Crispy bangs, highlights, tank tops on top of tank tops from Hollister; she looked amazing! Still, neither of us could really shake the insecurities we developed in our early years at school. Call it trauma bonding or even codependency, we felt safe when we were together.

Her new look in tenth grade, in fact, inspired my *Say Anything* moment. OK, I didn't have the stereo, but standing outside her house in the pouring rain, I shot my shot.

I'm outside, I texted.

lol it's raining, she responded.

I know but I just wanted to come here and tell you something.

I'm watching American Idol with my parents.

I didn't respond and walked home through our neighborhood. I knew she liked me. How could she not? I'd become a PacSun-wearing hottie with puka shells around my neck. We both grew into our bodies, our personalities, but we were still the DUFFs (designated ugly fat friends). My nickname transitioned from poison ivy boy to big-ass-alien-head while Ashley became *Who's-your-friend?*

I called her Rain.

Once I got home and dried off, I signed on to AOL.

Beeep beep beep crshhhhh shhh beep beep beep.

Welcome!

I went to the only place I knew where I could express myself freely in the privacy of my own home. My public blog that everyone would read.

9:45 PM

Feeling defeated.

UGH, my crush RAIN totally rejected me tonight. I'm so sad :(maybe I have a better shot with Avenger or Missile. Whatever, don't find me.

Closing the window, I navigated to the Favorites Menu and clicked on Bubble Pop. The page loaded slowly, one image at a time, with the bold HTML header reading *Men Kissing Men*. I scrolled for a bit, frequently looking around to make sure my parents didn't wake up before shutting down.

I gave people unique nicknames on my blog, writing longingly about my male crushes, and being obvious enough with girls that people would think I was… normal. I was dying to be found out, but with *Will & Grace* and Matthew Shepard's murder dominating the queer narrative at the time, I didn't want to be a gay best friend, or worse, end up dead.

Missile was Michelle Missel, a senior cheerleader. Avenger was a male cheerleader with a red Dodge Avenger, the hottest car, and the hottest girlfriend.

Goodbye!

The next day, everyone at school knew that my "RAIN" post was about Ashley, and she found me immediately.

"I had no idea," she said.

"No idea?" I shot back, "You used to have the biggest crush on me. This isn't new."

"I know, but we're best friends," she said.

"It's cool, we can be friends, I just…" I gripped my books wrapped in brown paper bags, "it's cool."

And it WAS cool. We were at the phase in high school where we drank vodka and Orange Lavaburst in a McDonald's parking lot, smoking weed in the woods. The two of us would end the nights together parked outside my parents' house. We didn't need a relationship to ruin our friendship, and people were starting to like us, so it was probably best not to cause any drama.

Senior year came, and Ashley and I were both dateless to prom. We had numerous crushes since the rain incident. On a random trip to the mall, she looked at me in the Dollar Tree and said, "Should we just go together?" as I fidgeted with deflated foil balloons. The girl who rejected me earlier in high school was now asking me to prom?

What I wanted to say was *I want to go with Jon. Or maybe Andy, with the red Dodge Avenger, remembers me even though he graduated three years ago, and he'll come pick me up and take me away to another life.* What I said was "Let's do it!"

And we did the whole thing, including hot afternoon dates to the tanning salon. After one session, the two of us walked our sweaty bodies, dripping in oil, to Ashley's car, eyelids white from the peepers, and drove home.

"I can't wait to get out of here," I said.

"These are the best years of our lives!" Ashley argued.

"I really hope not," I said from the passenger seat.

"Is this really that bad?"

"This is great, I didn't mean that." But I did mean that. I meant that I hated pretending to fit in with these people just so they'd only *jokingly* make fun of me, as friends did. I hated that I couldn't go to prom with a boy, and even if I could, I wouldn't be able to find one.

I remember being in Men's Warehouse with my dad getting measured and sized for my suit. I knew Ashley would be wearing black, and I'd go with a classic look, but I leafed through the different patterns: paisley, checked, striped, and all the different colors. I imagined myself in all purple to contrast the tan, diagonal stripes on my tie.

"You look so grown up!" Dad said, while I looked at myself in the three-way mirror in my fitted black-and-white suit. "Ready for the big day?"

"What? Oh, yeah, I guess. We'll have fun." When we get to prom weekend afterwards, I thought, looking forward to shutting my thoughts off with weed and alcohol.

I turned away from the mirrors, taking one more look at the colors, and wondered if I'd get married one day. When I came out to my dad years later, he said *I'd love you even if you had three heads.*

It was raining on prom night, but this time, I had an umbrella and Ashley let me inside. She looked beautiful when she opened the door. Bangs straightened, falling right below her eyebrows, wearing an elegant black dress. We both looked like we spent the last two months on a beach vacation. We knew each other so well, but I was still nervous. Our parents knew each other and photographed us inside the house since it was so rainy outside.

"They're so cute," Ashley's mom said.

"I know, and they hang out every day!" my mom responded. "One day they're definitely going to get married."

"We will NOT," Ashley said coyly.

"Never say never!" I shot out, knowing that we would never, but that we could.

*

When we walked into the hall, it was a wide-open lobby with sprawling stairs that spiraled to a second floor. The girls wore gowns, holding their clutches to show off their nails, while the boys donned the prom uniform of a tux, just with different colors and patterns on their ties to match their dates. It was a beautiful venue, the kind of place I hadn't really been in before. The same kind of place about which I'd proudly declare, "You couldn't catch me dead getting married in one of these."

I don't remember much about the evening itself, even though Ashley and I vowed to attend it sober. I remember the tiny flower-shaped butter that

I thought was soap or chocolate, waiting in line for photographs, dancing to Missy Elliot and Gwen Stefani.

When the DJ finally played the class-voted prom song, Eve 6's "Here's to the Night," Ashley and I slow-danced, along with many of the others.

So denied, so I lied
Are you the now or never kind?
In a day and a day love
I'm gonna be gone for good again
Are you willing to be had?
Are you cool with just tonight?

Listening to the words, I thought about how I lied to Ashley, to our friends, and about who I was, what I wanted. I saw the one openly gay kid in our class dancing with a girl. I saw Jon dancing with a girl.

"We'll stay in touch when you go to college, right?" Ashley asked with her hands draped around my shoulders.

"Ashley, we will always be friends," I said, pulling her closer, "and we have all summer!"

"You're right. I love you."

"I love you too." Among the sea of slow dancers, who all tried to stand out by looking the same, I found a friend.

Right before my senior year in college, I would come out of the closet. Sitting in Ashley's car one night outside of my parents' house, we chatted in the dark, red glow of the car radio. We were still close, but I started to drift toward new people, the possibility of a new life and identity drawing me further from who I was in high school.

"I have something to tell you," I said.

I half expected her to stop me before I started: *YES! YES! I do, I will, I've always been in love with you, too!* But when I said the words, she started crying.

"Why didn't you think you could tell me?" She looked at me in the rear-view mirror.

"You never asked," I said. I don't know if I would have even told the truth if she had asked. We cried, awkwardly hugging across seats in the car.

"I'm not going to just be your gay best friend, you know, I'm at least 40 percent straight still!"

"Come on, we can be Will and Grace," she started to soften.

"Will isn't even the gay one!"

She was my wingman to the first gay bar I ever went to, The Den in New Brunswick, where I'd make out with a boy in the bathroom. Where a bear would flick my nipple and say, "You'll do just fine out here."

Years later, Ashley and I smoked a cigarette outside the kitchen at a fancy venue, much like prom. She wore her long, heavy bridal gown while I wore a suit with a blue tie and vest to match the other groomsmen.

"Only us," she said, lighting up.

She still had bangs, just parted to the sides. I had a boyfriend.

"Do you think they're wondering where we are?" I asked, flicking an ash.

"Who cares," she said.

"Who cares," I agreed, and I think I finally meant it.

"A foot out the door"
"... itseems like
no one
has a
good time
at prom."
NAIL
POLISH
AKM25

Just Like the Movies

Ari Figueroa

A discounted dress, just a little too big
My dad knew a guy
A misfit group that nobody asked
My aunt bought the corsage
I wanted my life to be a movie
So they called me an optimist

Latin music and a sad candy bar
But I would barely dance
Too hung up on not being "Hispanic enough"
Quarter-Rican
I watched my theater friends dance with the boys I liked

There wasn't a spot for the standard cliche photo
Or a punch bowl waiting to be spiked
There wasn't a band on a stage
We had spent the budget on a country club hall
We should've just used the gym

The beginning at the end
Done with the night, putting on my shoes
"Wind Beneath Your Wings" finished out the DJ set
I used to think that song was cheesy
Back when I took myself so seriously
Before I actually watched *Beaches*

He came over and *Cinderella*-style fastened my silver kitten heel to my left foot
We had been fighting for weeks, maybe longer
About what I don't remember
Because this was my movie moment
Internal cameras rolling, the lights changed
And for the longest time, this was the only part of prom I remembered

I let the problems disappear without apology
Because this was my rom-com

The beginning of the end
He knew I craved a cinematic life
So he peppered our friendship with grand gestures
And they always overruled the negatives
Red flags are just flags when you're wearing rose colored glasses
Or so the owl said

I didn't know how friendships could be toxic
All the TV specials made sure you knew abuse was physical
But it was all the little things that pulled me to reality
The gifts I got him and had to keep for myself because they weren't good enough
The cats I left because he made sure I knew that he was a better caretaker
The security deposit with a portion missing because I hadn't done a good enough job repainting the room when I left

It started with a shoe, it ended with a foot out the door
Sometimes memories are just lessons learned
Sometimes moments are just a moment
And sometimes a movie prom is just a mediocre party

Sitcoms, Teen Movies, and How One Second-Generation Immigrant Teen Stumbled Through Prom Season

Lakshmi Gandhi

It's a truth universally acknowledged that if you come from a South Indian immigrant family, the majority of your knowledge of prom comes from the classic '90s teen sitcoms.

Well, that was a truth universally acknowledged in my house, anyway.

"You know, if you watch TV, it seems like no one has fun at prom," my mother said during the lead-up to mine. "Blossom didn't have fun."

Blossom, for those of you who were not Xennials immersed in '90s pop culture, wasn't a family friend or coworker's daughter or a neighbor or anything. She was Blossom Russo, the teen from California played by Mayim Bialik in the titular sitcom that ran from 1990 to 95.

And my mom was right—Blossom didn't have a good time at the prom. (Her dad wouldn't let her go to the prom with the older boy that her big brother Joey warned her off from! Can you believe it?!) It's also true that Dana from *Step by Step* (1994) was jilted because her date decided to return to an ex, and Kelly Kapowski from *Saved by the Bell* (1990) almost had her prom night completely ruined because her dad lost his job. Money was just too tight to send her to the iconic end-of-high-school event.

For a middle schooler (and her family members) who had no point of comparison, prom sounded very treacherous indeed. It got worse when that middle schooler grew up a bit into an even more anxious teenager. Prom then became more than a distant hypothetical—it was an event that loomed on one's social calendar. Even at the time, instead of feeling like an exciting coming-of-age moment, it felt strange and unfortunate, like a little weird cloud of dread edging closer and closer on the horizon.

Here, I feel I must add this, as an Indian American writer sharing a story about coming of age: My parents would have loved to have had a life-of-the-party, social butterfly of a daughter. Instead, the universe gave them a firstborn who, by age 15, knew entire sections of *Jane Eyre* by heart and felt that no one could understand her except white male singer-songwriters born in the Northern English city of Manchester between 1959 and 69. Her inner voice was, and is, a very, very earnest being. For which I am now grateful. That being said, this was neither a personality nor a family at large that was prepared for a party with poofy dresses and songs that would fit on a "Now That's What I Call Music" compilation.

One could only wish there were a guidebook or map, or even a set of flashcards to lead us through what to expect at prom.

It might go something like this:

Prom is expensive. Literally and psychologically.

Growing up on Long Island, one got pretty used to outward signs of wealth and conspicuous consumption. Or so you initially thought.

Then came the lead-up to prom—and with it, talk of hair! And makeup! And limos. Did you know people paid attention to the YEAR the limo was issued?

You did not—until you were quickly set straight by a girl in your friend group.

It remained odd. You were one of only a handful of Indian kids in your grade, and all of them somehow seemed much more socially adjusted than you. Despite that, and despite the fact that you didn't even have a date—after all, asking your friends and family for introductions was like an unfathomably slippery slope for your little second-generation self—you were determined to go.

"This is all so ridiculous. It costs *how* much?" your dad asked.

He paid for it anyway.

The day of, your mother took you to the salon inside JCPenney to get your nails done. It was the first time either of you did such a thing, and it felt fancy and indulgent. The manicurist seemed both delighted that these were your prom nails and disappointed that you picked such a simple color.

She was also eager to talk. Did you know her daughter? The girl was two years younger than you and at the same school. As she shaped your nails, the manicurist shared her thoughts on prom dresses and limos and all those things that you yourself learned about only just weeks ago.

"But I don't know how I'll ever afford it," she added.

You sensed your mother getting secondhand stress as prom affordability became a running theme throughout the appointment, probably because she was recalling her own childhood and the things she never had.

"She said she couldn't afford it so many times," your mom noted in the car on the way back. "This should never be so expensive that the children of working people can't go!"

She shook her head for the rest of the ride.

If you are an awkward misfit the day *before* prom, please prepare yourself for the fact that you will be a misfit the day *of* prom.

It turned out that deliberately embracing a contrary, introverted streak and being the kind of teen who spent all their money on CDs by obscure Britpop bands (Blur! Travis! Menswear!) was not great preparation to be fun at parties.

No attempt to tame your unruly eyebrows, put yourself in a gown, or find a lip color that genuinely works for a South Asian complexion would actually work. Because if your first impulse when asked "What kind of music are you listening to right now?" was to start riffing on how Pulp's 1995 single "Common People" was the perfect illustration of the class differences that existed in the post Thatcherite Britain—it was very unlikely that you would ever have a Rachael Leigh Cook in *She's All That* moment.

Cliches are even more true than you first thought.

Despite your uneasiness, you would remain oddly determined to go to prom. But *why?* you even asked yourself. Because you couldn't let them win, your inner voice whispered back. You had to try. You might not have been Rachael Leigh Cook or Molly Ringwald or someone from a long-forgotten sitcom, but you had to at least try. After all, how could you have a grand moment—maybe someone would notice you; maybe they'd tell you that they found you secretly delightful!—if you didn't show up?

You had to be the main character of your story.

Prom turned out to be fine. Not spectacular. Not scary. Just fine. Then, in the blink of an eye, high school would end, and you'd marvel at how brief it all was.

But just as you went to prom without fully knowing why, you also would diligently go to reunions, your anxiety rising to tenth-grade levels despite the years of therapy and degrees since. And, because you never grew out of the habit of awkwardly stumbling into conversations with people upon arriving at parties, you found yourself unexpectedly in a corner with a former lab partner. Her intense bullying of you was next-level personal and you will not—despite hundreds of writing classes and a journalism degree—ever be able to write the multi-month episode down.

It's important to pretend to be normal, your inner voice whispered.

"Oh, hi, [redacted]! It's Lakshmi."

Curiously, she somehow couldn't seem to look at you. It felt odder than even those mortifying moments in middle school, which you immediately pushed below the surface.

"I was mean." The words seemed to rush out of her mouth involuntarily and hesitantly. Unlike you, [redacted] was never hesitant as a teenager. You were momentarily stunned.

Then, inexplicably, you said the following: "That's ok," while nodding. "I was really shy then."

[redacted] didn't look well. Your brain was occupied with whether to get a glass of water from the bar or scan the room to see if anyone there had become a doctor. You did not have time to wonder why you essentially just excused your tormentor.

Luckily, [redacted] seemed to recover. "Well, you're not shy now."

You quickly realized it was time to close the curtain on this weird awkwardness and rushed off, chit-chatting with people the way regular people apparently did.

That was weird. You'd think after the reunion, before distracting yourself by thinking of all the concert tickets you'd like to buy, all the experiences you've chosen for yourself. Then you'd walk to the subway in the brisk air, quietly marveling about how, against all the odds, you are *All That*, after all.

"nothing new there..."

AKM 25

"what do you mean. of course you want to go."

BHS, Class of '91

KC Trommer

After a little sidebar with Andy before we left for prom, my father ushered us out to the lawn, holding the camera in one hand and waving us out with the other. Andy, my brother-in-law's younger brother, was Hollywood cute, older than me, and had driven his sad Datsun right up 95 all the way from New Haven to take me and my red tulle and black velvet dress to prom. Peakes Auditorium was dim under the haze of Aqua Net that let the cheerleaders shape and hold the double claw of their bangs in place. Jody and I stood back while the DJ played Guns N' Roses, nothing new there, and watched Andy dance with all the cheerleaders, Cher, Becky, Meghan, and all three Lizzes, but not me. I didn't want to dance to that shit music anyhow and soon I was never going to have to see those girls again. Afterwards, we loaded up Andy's car with everyone he didn't dance with and wound our way to the top of Cadillac Mountain to see the sun rise over Frenchman Bay. There would be no kissing. Years later, my father told me his warning to Andy: *If you touch her, I'll kill you*. And I see it now in the photos: Andy's nervous smile, his arm rigid around my shoulders before we drove away. In the backseat, the shadow of my father floated in and hovered, fatcatting all the way to Acadia exhaling Swisher Sweets clouds over his dominion.

A Prom Story

Jane Frances

There is so much media in American culture that revolves around prom: high school movies, high school TV shows, literally anything related to high school has the requisite "prom" theme. Spring 2005: I'm a senior in high school and too emotionally snarky and distant to want to go to prom. I saw myself as a Daria Morgendorffer, though I didn't have the combat boots or skirt to match; in fact, I hardly ever wore skirts or anything that seemed remotely feminine. I approached the idea of prom with much aloofness. I didn't care for it, too cool for it, and so deep in the closet that I couldn't even fathom asking someone, much less someone asking me.

By the time March rolled around, I assumed that I wasn't going to go. I had already thought of what I was going to do instead: browse stories on *fanfiction.net* or finally continue that "original" story I had stewing around on random scraps of looseleaf (essentially an adolescent knock-off of a *Final Fantasy* story).

I may not have had plans for prom, but that doesn't mean my mother didn't. I don't remember how the conversation came about; all I remember is being verbally strong-armed into going to Macy's at the Queens Center Mall to look at prom dresses (or dresses in general).

"When is your prom happening?"

"Not sure, sometime in June?"

"How can you not know?"

"I dunno, I don't think I want to go?"

"What are you talking about? Of course you're going to go!"

As an adult, it's easy to forget how little autonomy young people have over themselves and their personal lives, and I think this is doubly true for children of conservative Filipino immigrant parents who live in apartments in the five boroughs. A home isn't a home unless there's a giant portrait of *The Last Supper* hanging over the dinner table.

Standing in front of the mannequins decked out in flowy dresses of magenta and bright blue, I remember a sinking feeling in the pit of my stomach and a slight tightness in my chest that I would not understand to be gender dysphoria until decades later. The dread of looking at dresses and the thought of me being in them made me feel so uncomfortable. Memories of being a five-year-old crying before having to wear a frilly, itchy dress for a party I didn't even care about came flooding back.

"Aren't these dresses great? You should pick one!" my mom said.

Had I been braver or armed with the proper verbiage, I would have asked for a suit or a tuxedo of some sort, but I knew she wouldn't have given that a second thought. Girls wore dresses and boys wore suits.

"I don't know, maybe just something plain and black," I said, halfheartedly.

A simple black dress, size six (which I have not been since). I looked like I was ready for a funeral, but I didn't care; I just wanted it over with. I looked at myself in the dressing room, with mostly a smirk, trying to look like it felt normal to be in a dress, behind me, my mother, her eyes looking joyful.

Plans were made with a group of friends. Some were nerds like me, but most of us were in Key Club, the group where the main point of joining is "community service." I had initially joined because it was a good excuse to get out of the house outside of school hours. There was only one couple, Hanh and Terrence. The rest of us were friends, no dates, no boyfriends, just hanging out. Things were set up: a limo was rented (no idea who rented it), and we were all picked up from our houses by the limo. I hadn't realized so many of my classmates lived in East Elmhurst or Jackson Heights.

Eventually, we all made it to Terrace on the Park, or what I called "Titans Tower" because it was a huge T-shaped building in Flushing Meadows Park. It seemed so cool on the outside, but on the inside, it was a typical event space. It looked very much like a place where someone would have their wedding or sweet sixteen. I had imagined something modern and slick. Maybe decked out with exposed brick or millennial gray. Instead, it had fake beige marble accent pillars along with linoleum flooring, also made to look like marble. I hadn't really known what the setup for prom would be, but I knew I would feel uncomfortable, considering I wasn't much of a dancer, and "dancing" by high school standards was just grinding.

The night was a blur of dinner and some awkward dancing. Terrance was Filipino like me, and he quickly brought me to the dance floor where he twirled me around for a short while before I decided I wanted to sit back down. I thought it was nice of him to bring me out onto the dance floor, but I just felt awkward; it felt strange to be in the crowd, moving around, trying to imitate and follow along with what he was doing, moving around in this dress I didn't want to be in. I was only pretending to have fun while everyone else earnestly seemed to be.

Once I sat down, I looked over at the teacher chaperones dancing with each other, which I thought was strange, as I had never seen nor could I imagine my teachers in a setting outside of the classroom. Later that evening, I also watched everyone group dance the Electric Slide. I was a hipster before being a hipster was a thing: I hated the music but decided to shuffle around the dance floor occasionally with some of my singleton friends.

I felt a little out of place with all the sitting I had been doing. (Hipsters wanna be included too!) Photos were taken with other friends (some of which still survive in old Facebook posts), and we were all taken home by someone's older brother in their mid-'90s Land Rover by midnight.

I was never much of a party person, and the next day at school, some kids went up to me and said, "Oh, I heard you were in a dress and that you looked like a church girl!"

The embarrassment of being called a "church girl" was unbearable.

Oh God, just kill me now. Wait, do you even exist?

"I'm so surprised you went to prom, I thought you were gonna stay home!"

So did I.

"Did you like prom?"

Man, I hate y'all.

I mustered a fake smile, "Yeah, it was OK. I hate that dumb Usher song, though."

"Yeah? It's so overplayed. That 'Gasolina' song is also wack."

As a teen, I couldn't figure out why my mom was so adamant about having me go to prom despite my lack of desire. With the experience of adulthood, I see that she had never had that experience growing up, and I think she wanted me to have what she didn't. She grew up in a very poor family in what was once a rural area of the northern Philippines. She rarely talks about her past, but I assume she had some sort of filial duty to deal with, which meant she could not go to her (what she would call) "Junior/Senior Prom." She came from a poor family and was sent away at the age of eight to take care of her much younger cousins. Think *Jane Eyre*, but worse, because it's in a colonized country. I think she wanted to know that I was experiencing something she couldn't.

I suppose it's good to have memories of prom, and it was nice to not have had the internal pressure to perform or look good: I was at prom for reasons that weren't entirely my own and didn't have a "date" to worry about. I was responsible for the fun I had. I should have let myself go a little more, felt less scared on the dance floor, and been more open to just cutting loose and letting things happen. If I could do it differently, I would have gone in a suit. Though I don't think I would have been able to handle all the stares and questions from my peers.

People like to think that living in NYC is progressive, but folks forget that there are pockets of conservatism everywhere, especially if one's parents are from a conservative country. Even though I knew that my city was a liberal place, it definitely didn't feel that way as I was growing up. It's hard for a teenager to not only have their own authentic voice but also be unafraid to use it. I couldn't imagine myself being able to break away from my mother's sphere of influence as a teen. Now that I'm grown, it's nice to see how much I have changed.

I attended my 20-year high school reunion several weeks ago. It was good to see people I went to school with, now that I am the person I want to be: free of the closet and rigid gender norms, and in a profession that is able to sustain my life (high school English teacher, of all things). I saw some familiar (and unfamiliar) faces, had some beer, ate some snacks, and did some small talk.

The senior class president (who I think now works in real estate) said, "You know, you were so cute in high school, and if I knew you were interested in guys, I would have asked you out!"

I looked at him incredulously, flatly replied, "Oh really? That's kinda funny," and refilled my glass with a nearby pitcher.

It's always funny to me when a man admits a crush or some sort of attraction because I never expect it. I guess my gayness was very obvious then, too, despite my efforts to conform. I was free of anxiety and the constant pit of worry that came with being a teenager for me.

There was a raffle to win a Labubu. I didn't win. I did, however, partake in a blunt that someone passed around. Unfortunately, weed makes me feel anxious, so I left before sunset, went straight to my apartment, and cleaned as if my mom was coming over. Nothing like a clean apartment fueled by the existential dread of a parent coming over. Some things you can't really outgrow. In this case, the fear of a parent yelling at you for having an unkempt space.

In the 20 years since prom night, I've grown and changed into a person I couldn't have imagined as a high schooler. I have a place of my own, I work a job that is mostly fulfilling (but incredibly exhausting), and I don't keep social connections that don't bring me joy. As a teen, I couldn't envision what adulthood could be like. What freedom truly is: free from the worry of what others might think and how they see you. Prom wasn't the be-all and end-all of adolescent life, but a blip in the pattern of one's life: another signpost with which to compare oneself.

A bookend to high school and teenage life, a memory to take into adulthood.

THE WAY WE WERE
"YESTERDAY..."
#1 matchmake
"...Same WORD AS TOMORROW."
AKM

Some Kind of Metaphorical

Abeer Y. Hoque

I learned about America
through '80s movies
puffy pastel dresses
awkward front door greetings
the girl comes down curved stairs
the boy waits in a too-big suit
the dad shakes hands
the mom takes a photo
everyone is white, everyone is rich

I thought it was so romantic at the time
though now I want to know
why did the tomboy drummer girl want
blood diamond earrings so bad?
why did the pretty boy use
his college savings to buy them?
why was everything so heteronormie?

I wanted to already be at prom
but I didn't want go to prom
going to prom would mean
someone would have to ask (me)
and I would have to have (all the things)
a white-appropriate outfit
a white-appropriate body

Thank god for the kids these days
off to prom with their bestie squads
still corsaged and boutonnièred
draped in satin and velveteen
no one hoping or waiting
to be asked or answered
everyone dancing with everyone else

Where's brown John Hughes
to make an '80s prom com
set in a cramped foyer crowded with shoes
embroidered kamis, flowing dhupatta
a date with an ill-conceived mustache
matching hers, recently Naired yellow
not the date she wanted but the one who dared
the father adamantly opposed
but strong-armed into silence
the mother patting too light powder
onto too light foundation
and off the two go into the evening of yesterday
which as every Bangali knows
is the same word as tomorrow

Prom Stories: My Mother's and Mine

Mary Lannon

I don't know who my mother went with or what she wore or where her prom took place. Instead, my mother's only prom story is about setting my father up for his prom, which she did not attend. This lacuna in her life story stands despite the fact that my mother regularly told detailed stories of her life. Here's how she mostly tells the prom story about my dad (Joe Lannon):

When I was a junior, John Malone, the guy I was going with, asked me to get a date for Joe Lannon. So, I asked my best friend, Maureen, if she would go. Maureen said, "Arggh, that Joe Lannon never talks." But still she agreed to go. And so we go on this double date so that your father can ask Maureen to go to the prom. On the date I'm talking, Maureen's talking, my date's talking, your father doesn't say a word. It was all set up. All he had to do was ask. Finally, we pull up to Maureen's house, and your father walks Maureen to the door and at the door he says, "Will you go to the prom with me?" And she says, "Yes." And that was it. The only words your father spoke the whole night.

Despite differences in time and place, my own prom story shares commonalities with this one. First, my mother played matchmaker in both. She got me my date, Leo, when she ran into his mother at the supermarket. Second, and part of the reason that I was in need of my mother's help, is that, like my father, I was very shy during high school.

My mother tells her anecdote, I think, because it's funny, and because I'm sure when she was setting up that prom date, she never imagined that she'd marry my father.

Now I see that this story says a lot about the world my parents grew up in: Northeast Philadelphia in the late '50s. For one, everybody in the story is Irish American and Catholic. For another, they are tight-knit: everybody cooperated to get my dad a date, even Maureen, who did not relish the idea of going to the prom with my dad. The story also shows the conventions of the time. My mother and John Malone couldn't just arrange the prom date. They had to arrange for my father to formally ask Maureen.

They all lived in distinct neighborhoods, which everyone then identified by the name of the Catholic parish they attended. So, my mother and Maureen lived in Corpus Christi, and my father and John Malone lived in St. Columba. They went to adjoining large, all-boys or all-girls Catholic schools.

Unlike my mother, I have never regularly told my prom story. After all, mine doesn't involve a future husband. But now I see that in a different way, my prom story portends my future and tells about my hometown: 1980s Stroudsburg, PA.

Stroudsburg touted itself as "the Gateway to the Poconos" back then, a Poconos which once claimed to be the Honeymoon Capital of the World (take that, Niagara Falls!). Whatever its renown, it was a small resort town with a one-story mall and a dying Main Street. My world could be said to be even smaller than the town because I went to Notre Dame Jr./ Sr. High School, which had a graduating class of 39 students. Awfully small and tight-knit in a way that might have been similar to my parents' neighborhoods.

I could interpret my mother's prom story as a metaphor for the relations between men and women in her generation. Because she doesn't tell a story about herself but about my dad, it shows that men were the main characters and women the supporting players. As a teenager, that's the story I'd have told about my mother: someone who didn't challenge the norms of her time. I did not want to be like her, a housewife, but wanted a career, a husband, and an equal split of household chores. All of which I believed would be easily achieved. Feminists opened the door, and I just had to walk through it.

But I might have considered myself a rebel back then more to cover for my lack of social success. After all, rebels are not people who don't fit in because they are shy, but people who don't fit in because of heroic stances or because they are different in a good way. My best friend and

I declared ourselves spiritual, not materialistic people. We were both church-going Catholic girls with fathers devout enough to be eucharistic ministers at church. This background was part of the reason I was such a people-pleaser at that age (though, really, people-pleasing in our culture comes easily to 17-year-old-girls, religious or not).

We valued spiritual goods like friendship, love (romantic love heavily, as we were teenage girls), and morals derived from our love of God—unlike, we said, most of the kids we went to high school with. They were materialistic and valued Izod shirts, Jordache jeans, and Etienne Aigner purses, and cared about the types of cars (DeLoreans were out of their reach, but still, they could dream) that many would get on their 16th birthdays. Never mind that we didn't exactly have a choice to be materialistic, as neither of our families could afford designer clothes or a new or used car.

I'd often ask my mother why she didn't have an engagement ring. Her reply was always the same: *Your father couldn't afford one. And it's not what was important.* From other comments, I got the feeling that she looked a little down on women who cared about having a diamond and even more so on those who talked about the size of their diamond. It's possible my mother considered herself a rebel among diamond-obsessed women.

Another story from her early married life that my mother tells reflects her non-materialistic values: *We kept our money in a sock. When the sock funds started to run low, we hoped someone was going to get paid soon.*

In these and other stories, my mother emphasized the romance rather than the difficulties of their straitened circumstances. My mother once told her sister, "Joe wants me to cut costs further, but I don't think I can."

Though I saw myself as a rebel who was nothing like her parents, maybe I learned these spiritual attitudes from my mother.

My rebel facade also showed early signs of cracking. I really wanted a boyfriend, for example. I envisioned this boyfriend as spiritual and not materialistic as well, but it was still a pretty conventional desire. I also loved shopping at the mall (again, the '80s). And I don't think the sales my best friend and I sought out at Fashion Bug or Casual Corner or Hess's were evidence of our spiritual outlooks. I also loved having my makeup done or shopping for a pretty dress for church. Though I enjoyed these activities, I also considered them frivolous, especially compared to math and science classes that would lead me to a better (read a masculine) career. Third-wave feminism and girl power were only on the horizon, and my understanding of feminism was minimal.

I did feel torn about going to the prom senior year. Proms did not seem to comport with rebellion. Still, as the event got closer, and one by one all my friends and classmates decided to go, I ended up really wanting to go to the very girly, very materialistic prom. I especially didn't want to be the only girl not to go.

To be fair, '80s culture might have been as pro-prom as it was pro-mall: Molly Ringwald in *Pretty in Pink* rebelled and went to prom.

The big problem was that I didn't have a date. Enter the supermarket encounter between my mother and Leo's mother.

Leo was not my first choice for a prom date. But my high school crush had a girlfriend, and most of the other desirable guys were taken. I was at home, probably watching a TV show like *Family Ties* or *Cheers*, when, thanks to my mother, Leo called me up. "Hello, Mary, would you like to go to the prom with me?" was the extent of the conversation. Because I didn't have a date already, the nice thing to do was to accept, so I accepted because I was a nice girl, a people-pleasing girl. Maybe not so different from Maureen in my mother's prom story.

Leo's most prominent characteristic was his slicked-back, 1950s-style hairdo. He also walked with his head down at a pace that could be described as languid. None of the clean-cut guys I went to high school with had such a hairdo. I dare say that very few teenagers in the late 1980s sported such a style. Rebel that I was, I could have found Leo's unusual style charming or brave. But I did not. I had always found Leo odd, though not odd as in embarrassing, but more odd, as in significantly differing from the norm. As for my classmates' reactions, Leo had gone to school with many of them since first grade (I joined in seventh grade), so Leo's unusual style was more like a piece of old purple furniture that's been there so long you don't really see it. Leo, then, was not popular, but he was not bullied.

Still, once Leo became my prom date, his oddness took on new dimensions: a light seemed to shine down upon his quirks. I told myself looks were not important; what mattered was inside. Regardless, I couldn't help but see that a date with Leo was not the stuff of dream prom fantasy; this was not *Pretty in Pink*. At least I was going to the prom. I would not be the only girl who didn't go.

Looking back at it, I think my favorite part of prom was wearing the dress. My mother came with me to buy it. Ordinarily, shopping with my mother was frustrating for both of us, as she steered me to more conservative clothes. Though the difference between her conservative ideas and my less conservative ones was not vast, the difference maybe between a skirt above the knee and one slightly below. No punk rock black mini, Doc Martens, or leather clothes were available. In fact, I had no idea what punk rock was at the time, as my classmates glorified classic rock and dissed country as if only two genres existed. Oh, how small a world it was!

Most of the prom dresses available in Stroudsburg were more romantic than sexy. Self-conscious about my body, I chose a romantic one, a magenta gown with a high-waisted sash and flouncy sleeves.

Leo arrived to pick me up, sitting in his truck at the top of the driveway, which sloped steeply down to the house. Today, or even then, some people would see the truck as an unusual vehicle for prom. I don't remember anyone making any remarks about it. Maybe because trucks were so commonplace in Stroudsburg, or maybe because we were practical-minded people who saw the truck as a means of transportation to the main event and not part of the main event.

I stood in the living room, wearing the magenta gown, and waited for Leo to come down the driveway. Then I waited some more. There was discussion. "That's Leo, isn't it?" "Up there in the truck?" Our house had no lawn in front, and tall pine trees obscured the view of the road, so we craned our necks out various windows to try and see who was in the truck. More minutes passed. Leo still sat in his truck at the top of the driveway.

After more discussion, it was decided, or maybe my brother volunteered to go get Leo and tell him he had to come down, that pictures had to be taken. My brother went up, and Leo came down. He was wearing a tux; he had bought a corsage. We took pictures out on the driveway in front of the rhododendron under the tall pine trees.

During our drive to the resort where the prom was held and while there, I tried to engage Leo because, as noted, I was a Catholic schoolgirl and, therefore, believed that Jesus was within everyone. I tried to get Leo to talk, and he did, with one- or two-syllable answers. I felt frustrated, but also bad for feeling frustrated because "helping others was its own reward," and yet I felt no reward.

Proms are long. There's little to do after the meal but dance. So, it took a while, but I coaxed Leo out onto the dance floor. The DJ spun an '80s mix: songs from artists like Bon Jovi, Cyndi Lauper, Van Halen, John Cougar, and Led Zeppelin. Our class song was "The Way We Were."

Dancing wasn't exactly Leo's thing. If you remember a scene from the sitcom *Happy Days* where The Fonz bobbed while four girls danced around him, that was dancing with Leo, except I was the only girl circling him. I felt sort of silly, but I also felt that I was making the best of a not-so-great situation.

As we moved on and off the dance floor, rumors flew of after-prom parties. My friend and I went to the ladies' room to discuss. The words "ditching Leo" were used. Part of me felt bad about this. But I did not think I could spend a few more hours trying to get Leo to do things like utter one or two words. Another part of me felt gleeful about doing the "wrong" thing for once. I can't remember who my friend's date was. But the plan was to ditch our dates, and then she would pick me up, and we'd go to the after-prom parties together.

At least, I think that was our plan. In the end, we stopped at my friend's house and talked to her mother for a longer time than I wanted to. By the time we got to the after-prom party, it was wrapping up, and we didn't stay long. Overall, a letdown after all our plotting.

It's here that this prom story does portend my future. Ditching Leo was the first time I remember doing something I wanted to do rather than trying to please someone else. It wasn't so hard to go against my usual habit of mind because pleasing Leo was lots of work. What gratifies the people-pleaser, after all, and keeps them going is the pleasure of the other, and Leo didn't provide that.

While my mother was also taught to put men's needs first and did put my father ahead of herself more often than not, she didn't always do so. She tells a story about what her father thought about my dad, a graduate student (unusual, to say the least, in their set): *My father always said, "You watch. He'll keep going to school and you'll be supporting him your whole life."* But my mother didn't listen to this advice—rebelled against it even.

My mother also embraced feminism for her daughters, telling us that while her choices had been limited to teacher, nurse, or secretary, we could be anything we wanted to be, often adding that I'd make a good doctor or lawyer.

My mother became a nurse in part because her father was willing to pay her tuition. As my mother tells it: *Mr. Fisher said, "Why would you waste all that money? She's just going to quit and get married and have kids." But my father just said, "She wants to do it."*

I wish I could say that my prom story ended with both Leo and me having a nice enough prom experience. But this being high school, word got back to Leo that I'd ditched him. I know Leo wanted a conversation, and it took place a couple of days later in the weight room where Leo lifted. I think this desire and location were conveyed to me via a note.

As I approached the weight room, I felt nervous. Since I almost always pleased people, I wasn't used to being called out.

Leo and I stood on either side of a weight bench. Barbells and weights were scattered about the floor. The room, located under a stairwell, was not well lit and had no windows. I said something along the lines of "You wanted to talk to me?" Leo said he'd heard I ditched him and that was wrong.

I had to think fast to make it seem like I wasn't in the wrong, and I remember being impressed that I came up with: "But Leo, you really didn't seem to be having a good time," as the reason for my actions. It was for his benefit then, not mine.

"I was having a good time," he said, "and I would have gone to the after-prom parties with you."

I repeated that it wasn't clear to me that he was having a good time. The implication being that if it had been clear then, of course, I would have done what pleased Leo. And as I said it, I started to believe it was my real reason for ditching him. I apologized more. I think I let him have the last word, that what I'd done was wrong.

I know we did not speak about my pleasure, or debate whether I was having a good time or not. That didn't occur to Leo, or if it did, he didn't wish to entertain it. He felt wronged because his needs weren't met. And I knew that I needed to save Leo's ego and not hurt his feelings, so I didn't want to say I wasn't having fun. My feelings seemed less important.

The conversation I had with Leo that day in the weight room stayed with me for a few weeks, but then I moved on to a summer job and to college and to more people-pleasing. Eventually, all the people-pleasing became impossible to maintain (though that's another story), so I learned to please myself instead.

I still don't think my prom story is quite as good a story as my mother's. But I can now see that it's too easy to view me as the rebel and my mother as conventional.

There was no feminist movement for my mother to follow in working-class Philadelphia in the late '50s. Still, my mother carried out small rebellions: defying her father to take a chance on a guy with no money but big dreams, and not caring about having a diamond engagement ring, never mind its size. And my mother embraced feminism, not for herself but for me, and wanted me to have more opportunities. Perhaps my mother's rebellious spirit was partly shaped by her father, who paid for nursing school, not listening to his friend's view on the uselessness of doing so for daughters. My mother made other conventional choices: of marriage and motherhood, but that was true of most of her generation, the silent generation.

On the other hand, in the '80s, in small-town Stroudsburg, PA, I had a limited sense of feminism. At prom, for the first time, I put my desires above someone else's, taking baby steps away from people-pleasing on my way to an autonomy that allowed me to defy my parents' dreams for me and become a writer, a choice that pleased no one but myself. But I, too, was of my time. I thought I could just walk through the doors that feminism had opened and have it all: the husband, the children, and the career. Like many in Generation X, I found it wasn't possible to have it all, or at least to have it all without any compromise. In the end, I can be seen as one of "the '80s career women," emerging then like a new species of woman, one recognizable by her shoulder-padded suits, or in this case, her magenta prom dress.

"Because he loves me..."
Wesley sez: Kelly Jean is a hotty!
Welcome to ZOMBIE PROM
"my heart bleeds green"

Zombie Prom Queen

Lyrics by A King McCarty

I'm drained from being *perfect*
I'm sick from being *smart*
I'm dead inside from being that one person
Who will *do the right thing*
From the start.

I dream of being badass I'd rather be
THAT PUNK!
Wanna chew out all my enemies when
Someone tells me, *Girl, just suck it up.*
Just like a Zombie Prom Queen.
I wanna be a Zombie Prom Queen

I wanna shed this dress.
This costume that I'm in.
I'm a woman full of fury, and I
Just wanna win or lose,
On my own two feet,
But I'm way off beat.
Why can't I
Be me?

I'm not perfect, not nice or mean
I feel it all
Deep pain like a Scream Queen
I laugh it off
When I'd rather pick a fight.
Wanna bare my teeth
And take a big bite
Like a Zombie Prom Queen.
Be fearsome like a
Zombie Prom Queen

With a
Ballgown torn to tatters
And cobwebs coming out of my hair
One broken heel
and an attitude of *I don't care*
If you like me but won't somebody
Recognize me
Won't you love me as I am and not who I
could be

I'm just a Zombie Prom Queen

One short look
In a cursed bus station
And then three long months,
One brief tour of the nation
I have found someone
Who can see right through me
Past the curated form of this
Ghost girl goodie
It's gonna get weird
It's gonna be epic
Might break my heart or my
Back in the process
Not really sure how to do this right
I let go of *correct* and lean into delight

Then one day
You say:
We've got a date, My Queen,
Will you go to "Zombie Prom"
With me?

Now I'm in a
Ballgown torn to tatters
With cobwebs coming out of my hair
One broken heel and I'm

Stumbling down your stairs
Full of bad jokes
And good advice that you don't need
I'm a feminist Beetlejuice
My heart bleeds green
Is pretty and
Silly can be smart
When you let go of illusion
And chase your beat-less heart
Cause it led me to you
And a blood-filled basement full of
Dancing freaks
And joy with my Zombie Boy
I'm just a Zombie Prom Queen
A silly Zombie Prom Queen
A messed-up Zombie Prom Queen
A happy Zombie Prom Queen

When someone sees you as you see yourself
That's really the best
Kind of Love

The Boy

Kelly Jean Fitzsimmons

Spencer Flynn gave me a birthday present. Spencer Flynn gave me a birthday present. He gave me a present!! I had a crush on Spencer since I'd first joined drama. Tall and skinny with dark, dreamy eyes and a shock of brown, curly hair, he looked like Doogie Howser and was the person I most wanted to come to my birthday party. Because he loves *Star Trek: The Next Generation* as much as me. And because he's Spencer Flynn.

It had to be fate that the series finale of *TNG* was airing on May 23, my birthday. The same day Captain Picard and his crew were saying goodbye after seven years of boldly going where "no one has gone before" was also my big day. I was turning 17 years old.

"A Monday night! It never usually comes on Monday nights. And it's going to be two hours, not a two-parter, but two full hours. On my birthday."

I tried (again) to make my mother see why the *TNG* finale airing on my birthday was the greatest thing that ever happened to me.

"Monday's just not a good night for a party," she replied. "Can't we do it over the weekend? Make the *Star Trek* thing the theme?"

"No," I dug in, "it has to be on my actual birthday, and I'm only inviting people who super love *Star Trek*."

Trying to make my mother understand me may have been futile, but resistance was not. She ordered a sheet cake with the USS Enterprise etched in blue icing and watched in wonder as her living room filled with *Star Trek* fans of all ages: kids from school, one of my managers from the AMC movie theater where I worked as the concession stand supervisor, and a friend of mine from drama, who even brought his parents.

My heart lifted at the sound of the high-tech *vooooom cha-CAH* of the holodeck doors sliding open. Our collective breaths held until the first commercial break. Then the room erupted.

Was Picard's time-shifting back and forth between his first mission on the Enterprise, the present day, and 25 years into the future all a dream? No, it had to be real. But who were the strange people in raggedy clothing jumping up and down in the middle of old man Picard's future vineyard? Why were they laughing at him? My body buzzed with the uncut excitement of a sci-fi high—*anything could happen!*

Sure, it super sucked that Spencer couldn't come to my actual birthday party. Still, he gave me a present. And not just any present. THE present. A present that shows that, even though we've only ever been drama pals, and even though he is dating a Cool Drama Senior at another school, even though we're only juniors, the potential is there for him to love me. A part of him loves me. Even if he doesn't know it yet.

For my birthday, Spencer Flynn gave me an 8x10 glossy photo of Wil Wheaton as Ensign Wesley Crusher in his Starfleet uniform with a giant cartoon speech bubble glued onto it that read: *Wesley Sez: Kelly Jean is a hotty!* Here are my TOP FIVE reasons why my birthday present shows that Spencer secretly feels the same way about me as I do him:

1. This is a picture of Wesley Crusher. Not Picard. Not that I don't adore Picard. I do. What greater hero could a Drama Geek ask for than a starship captain brandishing a fencing foil who recites Shakespeare? That makes Picard the obvious choice. Or Data. Or Troi. But even though the cool thing is to hate on Wesley, I adore him. Because I adore Wil Wheaton. And Spencer knows I adore Wil Wheaton because he pays attention to me. Like you do when you love someone.

2. Where did Spencer Flynn get an 8x10 glossy photo of Wil Wheaton? The picture is not torn out of a magazine. It's thick cardstock. This means that Spencer went out looking for a picture of Wil Wheaton at the comic book store or the mall, just for me, for my birthday. Or, he was out somewhere, spotted the photo, and thought of me.

Either way, this means Spencer Flynn thinks of me outside of school. Because he loves me.

3. The first words, "Wesley sez:" are perfection because Spencer uses the funny "sez" but juxtaposes the slang word with the proper punctuation of a colon. This attention to detail illustrates he is both wacky and also into the intricacies of English and writing, like me, which means we are perfect for each other.

4. The last word, "hotty!" I about bit through my tongue to keep from screaming when I read, "Kelly Jean is a hotty!" First, my name is exactly how I want it to be. Both my first and middle names *Kelly* and *Jean*. I've been going by both for over two years, and my family still only calls me just "Kelly." Not only does Spencer respect my chosen identity, but he goes on to call me a "hotty!" Not cool, or awesome, or the dreaded hilarious, but a HOTTY! Punctuated by a goddamn exclamation point! The root of the word "hotty" is HOT. Out of all the words, Spencer Flynn picked "hotty." And I know I'm not hot. Not yet. But I will be when I lose the weight. And Spencer sees the secret hotty inside. The me I will be.

5. While it might not be apparent at first, the biggest clue to his love for me is the cartoon speech bubble. That bubble didn't just happen. No way Spencer somehow stumbled across a picture of Wil Wheaton with a white, ready-to-be-written-on speech bubble. He made that shit. He gathered supplies, sat down to trace it, cut it out, and glued the speech bubble to the photo. That's multiple steps. That's crafting. That is time taken out of your day. Spencer Flynn crafted a present for me, probably at his kitchen table where everyone could see him decree me, Kelly Jean, to be a hotty! Sure, I get that technically, within the conceit of the present, Wil Wheaton as Wesley Crusher is the one who "sez" the words. But Spencer thought of them, carefully inscribed them with a black sharpie, and he presented the sentiment to me in a perfectly tailored medium. *Why?* Let's say it all together now, shall we? BECAUSE HE LOVES ME.

Spencer's birthday present shifted me, like Picard, into the future where I could foresee the promise of our senior year. Next year, everything will be different.

When Spencer's girlfriend goes off to college, and when I lose the weight. When I really am a hotty. Senior year will be cur year.

To be together.

To go to prom.

To properly fall in love as we dance the night away.

NOW ARRIVING
P.R.O.M.
"all these lines connect"
NEXT STOP:
"ADULTNESS"
AKM 25

A *Meh* Prom

Sydney Beveridge

No fairytale prom.
Ask a friend to join me, please.
No drama either.

I primp anyway.
Flinch at each eyeliner stroke.
Ballet-pink nails chip.

A dress long enough
for my towering, slouched frame.
Satin blues soften.

Packs of teens roll in
performative limo rides.
Just a few photos.

Seventeen warped us.
Teen-movie sheen blinded us.
No Facebook burns, yet.

My mouth relishes
bites of molten chocolate cake
instead of a kiss.

We're gonna party
like it's nineteen ninety-nine.
All share the dance floor.

Cliques emulsify.
Separate as music ends.
Graduate apart.

Practice okayness.
Launch into my adultness.
Embrace the meh prom.

Prom oldies perk up
my meh grocery store runs.
Let's dance in the aisles.

Prom Night 1996

Vegas K Jarrow

I was born Vijay Ramanathan, also known as Vijay R. Nathan. At some point in the distant past, I felt pressure to perform to the expectations of others. Like I was an actor on a stage, and the responses I got from others were the applause or validation I needed to know I was doing the right thing. My second personality was born in the build-up to Senior Prom Night in early summer 1996.

Let's be clear, Junior Prom was fine. We had a prom, which I helped plan as one of the student government officials. That year, the officers all got together and planned out a cruise around Manhattan for the juniors of Tottenville High School. I had a special night as I talked with the other officers, even though most of the class was not in attendance. This felt very close-knit. I felt these years helped me understand that I could have an impact on the mainstream experience, even if it was not in the manner in which I would prefer. Everyone wants to impact everyone, and the herd experience is the dominant experience. But sometimes, if you yourself have a good experience and share it with your close allies and compatriots, then you've succeeded in your attempt to guide the mainstream narrative.

I was not a "cool" kid any more than any Indian American kid would be considered cool. I considered myself more of a "nerd" in the sense that I was high-achieving and very self-directed in my goals. I had made efforts to establish the very ambitious "Night at the Theater," a nonmusical drama event of two one-act plays, with me directing *No Exit* by Jean Paul Sartre and my friend H. directing *The Zoo Story* by Edward Albee.

I also tried to start a Model UN at school. Neither of these efforts met with much success. I did hold various positions within the student government but did not pursue that activity in my senior year. Much of the class ran that final year, and I knew I didn't stand as much of a chance with so much competition. I was also involved in more mainstream high school theater activities, although as part of the ensemble, not a main player. Despite this, I was nominated by my peers for "Most Likely to Succeed."

One blonde girl by the name of L., who had chosen me to talk to during the downtime of the classes, inspired me to send her a small bear and an anonymous Valentine's greeting. When she gave me the cold shoulder after the greeting was delivered, I didn't have the courage to directly claim it was me, nor ask her why she was so brutal about it. According to sources close to L., she didn't like that I had made it anonymous, but she also just wasn't interested in me that way. Obviously, she was not an ideal candidate for prom. I hoped she would find a good therapist to talk to in the future, and I went about my business of finding a date for prom.

When it came time to ask someone, I stayed true to my instincts, which were to ask whoever I was talking to at the time to prom. I asked a girl in my video class who declined but told me I'd go places in the world, and she was content to get a job at the local library, where she volunteered. As the future would have it, I ended up doing 15 years at the public library. I will say this was quite a flattering rejection. This inspiration for a job I had for so long also carried with it the curse of my own ambition to do and be more than just a librarian.

I then asked my friend and collaborator H., who was philosophically against proms and the dominant culture. She was confused when I asked her and used the excuse that, since she was not my "first" choice, which she figured out even though I tried to lie about that, she would stay true to her philosophy and decline. H. and I had a good friendship.

She was the one who introduced me to poetry and gifted me with a *Four American Poets* book that included Walt Whitman, Emily Dickinson, Robert Frost, and Wallace Stevens.

I realized I should lean into the dominant culture and try my best to be political about my choice of prom date. So, I asked M., who was a junior at the time but knew many of the theater group in the limo I had joined. She said yes, of course, to help me out of my difficult spot and just to enjoy the evening herself. I was exhausted after attempting to bring so many fellow students to prom and was glad to have received an acceptance.

I had multiple groups of friends over the four years in high school. It was only in my last year that I began to become closer to the drama clique. They were, as many of my friends indicated, a "bad influence" on me as far as being a high achiever and self-directed thinker. They were also a redirect away from my traditional trajectory, which makes my second personality emerge at this early stage. My second personality was one who tried to influence and have an impact on the dominant culture. Unlike H., I was interested in energy exchanges with the dominant culture, believing there to be a place for innovative thinkers to make a path for the herd to follow if they were charismatic enough or charming enough.

An elementary school teacher had told me, "You can't get through life on charm alone," but that statement seemed to teach me the exact opposite of its obvious contextual formulation. I decided this teacher didn't know what she was talking about, and I'd show her that I could get away on charm alone. Which is not to say I was born charming. Or that I achieved something akin to charming. Or that I had a charm thrust upon me. Sometimes you just practice charming until you are charming. I kissed the Blarney Stone on my junior year trip to Ireland and, well, that's all I have to say on that. There's a certain magic or understanding that comes with ancient traditions that cannot be translated into a mere common tongue. I trust the process.

At the pre-party, as we took pictures for the prom, my date, M., was invited by her mother to "Show them your slit, M."

Referring to the cut in her dress, which required her to spread her legs to maximize the display of the dress's features in the photograph. The arrangement of the date with M. felt very arranged, like my parents' marriage, only surprisingly less successful. M. felt accustomed to the limelight and attention, whereas I was a foreigner to the spotlight. Yearning for it but never receiving its full embrace. The yearning is what made the second personality all the more salient and delayed its full birth until years later.

We didn't really talk much that night, and when the ceremonies began, M. ran away very quickly to dance and be with the group of students present at the festivities. One of my good friends at the time, A., was also at the prom, and after a while of sitting around and listening to speeches, we navigated our way out into Manhattan, where the prom was taking place.

I have faint memories of that night, of wandering into a subway station chugging from a champagne bottle and trying out an old Irish trick to delay vomiting by massaging the lymph nodes in your neck.

I personally feel the prom is a great way to either begin an acculturation into dominant narratives about what we should be in our society, or a chance to know what we could be in our society when your acculturation hits the kind of snags that I experienced.

When it comes to drugs and alternative states of consciousness, high schoolers are ill-equipped to understand all the nuances of their own experience. By the time I reunited with my prom date, it was late in the evening, and M. was talking about her disappointment that someone had offered her "Buddha" to smoke up with them, and it was just marijuana and not something "cooler."

I had been born as Vijay Ramanathan, but at that moment, I felt a kick of my second personality. I feel sure that had I discovered marijuana with M. that night, I would have been able to sell it as cooler, but alas, that was a missed moment that probably would have taken a lot of work to set up on my part.

I wondered if, by smoking together, I could have elevated M.'s experience through my own understanding of non-ordinary states of consciousness, which was beginning to emerge from readings of the existentialists and other philosophies that challenged normative thinking. But of course, these are all silly dreams of a high school student who desperately wants to connect and influence the experience of others, rather than having their own experience guided by the norms of the masses, read as "asses."

If we are to explore the narratives, we will find that we can only find ourselves. Whether we are looking back or seeking what's to come, all these lines connect. At the end of the rainbow is who we are at the core. Prom is a significant rite of passage from high school, where we are guided to a more self-directed schooling in college or other alternative entry into adulthood. Going to Vassar challenged me. Suffice to say, the lineage that features a professor I met in my college years later ties itself back to many eons of my own genealogy of seekers and liberators who sought to integrate rather than destroy the dominant narrative. To influence rather than become engulfed in the ocean of nectar of experiences that are to be had in life.

From now on, I'm committed to higher paths that require clearly building off hard work and dedication to specific payoffs. If I had worked to connect with M., my prom date, and smoked Buddha with her, who knows what doors might have opened. Whether they be the doors of perception or not, I feel this missed chance was one that gave birth to my new expression of myself: Vegas K Jarrow, and for him to recover from and create a new path for myself and my agency for people who want to strive higher in life and enjoy their trip while they're here.

"Like talking to a DRAGON..."

"OLD SCHOOL HOLLYWOOD"

Firetruck Red

Anda Totoreanu

The house was half empty
when my parents separated
just bare rooms & my father's daily visits

he insisted I stop seeing you.

I told him if he laid a hand on you
I'd leave with you
I was only 18
& you moved in
with just your backpack
you promised to marry me

we shared a bed
no funny business I said
I wanted to wait until marriage
but your hands wandered up & down my body

when the day of prom came
we decided to wear firetruck red
a reference to our passion
I used to enjoy making out with you,
steaming up the car windows in your Camaro
parked in front of the neighbor's house

my mom refused to take me to prom
she said dancing was forbidden according to the Bible
but it was my one chance to feel "normal" in a house of chaos
so I chose you

I chose you even when my friends didn't let you come to the pre-party
they saw what I couldn't see—
that you were too old for me, too sad for me, too hopped up on drugs
you were never going to choose me

It was my dad who bought me my shoes
& my mom who came with me
to buy my dress even though she didn't approve
the lady from Craigslist gave me the dress for free
she said it fit me so well & her daughter had never worn it

when we got there my teachers told me
I looked like a movie star from Hollywood's classic era
& I beamed

I asked you to join me on the dance floor & you did
we laughed & you didn't know
where your feet or hands should go

For a moment it felt like it was only *us against the world*
& then suddenly my heart
sunk as I looked into your eyes
& realized you didn't really see me

I asked to leave
because I didn't want
everyone to know
they were right

& so we left
my dress barely fitting in your car
& went to Dairy Queen
for thick vanilla milkshakes & salty French fries

No Summer of Love

Aida Zilelian

I'll say I never liked the matching prom dress-cummerbund-and-tie thing and it was 1990 anyway, but my stomach lurched when Juan and Maria walked into the gymnasium. Cinderella-blue gown with satin gloves, Maria slipped her hand through Juan's arm as they crossed the room like royalty. *Hey Maria, just so you know, I was making out with Juan backstage during lunch last week and his hand was up my shirt.* He had said, "I'm going to be your first," after we straightened up to go to math. I was half in awe, but laughed it off anyway. Thinking what oracle shit he was trying to pull.

My friends Jen and Carol stood on either side of me, following my gaze as Juan and Maria sat at their table. We had decided to go stag with a few other girls and rent a limo. I lived around the corner and my Lebanese-Armenian mother was complaining for weeks about the sense of a limo. She had sewn me this ironically silver dress with a fitted bodice and a tulle sparkly gray skirt. Black suede heels and my hair blown out falling to the center of my back. Charcoal eyes and I looked edgy in the way I had always wanted to look, and by that, I mean a hybrid Siouxsie and the Banshees meets Sex Pistols fan edgy. But also, not suicidal looking. That was eighth grade. Back then, I was wearing clothes she had sewn from *McCall*'s magazine patterns. That was after long arguments at Jo-Ann Fabrics about the hemline of my skirts or our trips from the mall, returning empty-handed.

"They look so fucking stupid," said Carol. She was Polish and German with hair almost as long as Crystal Gayle's, and a wide smile. She was wearing a slinky midnight blue dress and didn't waste her time on high school boys. The rest of us were self-conscious and categorically uncool.

"They look miserable," said Jen. She and I had become friends in ninth grade on a school trip to Columbia University. We had snuck off during the student tour and bonded over our favorite Cure album. "He's such a dick. You could do so much better," she said, a long-standing opinion that never got under my skin because I knew she was right.

Juan was indefensible. He had a reputation for sweet-talking girls to go to the locker room during school dances, the goal being to kiss as many girls as possible without them finding out until the next day. I wasn't one of them; we had been kissing and stuff since the tenth grade. He was unabashedly rude to the teachers, telling our English teacher, Mrs. Elkind, once that he took long bathroom breaks because he hated her boring-ass class. No one spoke that way. It was a private school, and we followed a dress code of no sneakers, jeans or T-shirts. We muttered under our breath when a teacher pissed us off.

Also, he was a year behind. He had gotten left back in middle school, which surprised me because he was smart. Maybe it was because he had been a dick then, too. Juan's friends were a grade above ours. So Maria had already graduated. He had brought her to the prom because they had been dating since we were in the eleventh grade. Everyone had predicted they would break up again. Their relationship in high school had been a series of breakups, always in the hallway, Maria storming off in this actressy sort of way, and he'd be calling after her and then running. Yet here they were.

"Miserable," repeated Jen.

I squinted my eyes, trying to read their faces. Maria's lips were a thin, even line, and Juan was looking away from her, his chin resting on his fist, mumbling to himself. They'd had another fight.

Juan's eyes were swimming pool blue. Chlorine blue. And perfect floppy brown hair with one side of his head shaved. His mouth was sexy, which was a ridiculous thing to think—how did I know what a sexy mouth was, at seventeen? But I did. I loved kissing him, how slowly he moved his mouth against mine. Not desperate and sloppy like I was going to disappear or we were going to get caught. He didn't give a shit, and because he didn't give a shit, I didn't either.

So we got caught. It's not like I was going to college anywhere I wanted to go. Queens College was my default school because I wasn't allowed to dorm. When my mother told me that in the beginning of ninth grade, I took it in like I was watching a key fall into a well. I never bothered studying and my mother didn't bother telling me to. I was graduating with a solid eighty average.

So Juan. He was my longest crush. I didn't expect, hope, pray, that Juan would ask me to the prom. When I was with him, I wanted to be with him. But I never thought beyond that. Having Juan as my boyfriend would have been the equivalent of talking to a dragon. It made no sense.

I looked away from their table and then caught Jen's irritated look. Juan was leaning into Maria's ear, speaking to her slowly, very close to her ear. He kissed her face, then the corner of her mouth. She was resisting, trying not to smile. He touched her chin, tilted it toward him, and kissed her in that open-mouth soft way.

*

It was a few weeks before prom, a Tuesday after school, and I had left my last meeting with the Journalism Club. I had gone backstage in the auditorium to play the piano, knowing my mother was actually out of the house for once. She was in New Jersey visiting some woman who was here from *Bourj Hamoud*. (You should hear how she pronounces it. God, she leans hard into the Arabic 'H'.) I had at least an hour before she was back. The piano at home hadn't been tuned since years ago, when my mother had stopped taking lessons. The one backstage, behind the heavy blue curtains, was a beautiful Steinway that had barely been played.

I usually went through my songs. The ones I had written and loved to play because at home, I could only do that when no one was there. I wasn't even halfway through my first song when I heard his voice.

"Hey," he said. He was standing by the door of the backstage entrance. "What are you doing?"

I knew what that meant. He walked toward me, slipped his hands around my waist like he had so many times before, and kissed me. Then he stopped. I knew what this was. He liked teasing me into wanting more kisses and then pulling away.

He leaned into my ear. I felt his warm breath as he spoke, "I always want you. It's always you. It doesn't matter who I'm with." I didn't say anything, my insides dizzy. "What is it about you?"

I didn't answer. He would always kiss my face, the corner of my mouth, like he was doing now, and all around it until I leaned in for a kiss and he would pull back, grinning. Excited but holding back for leverage. When he looked at me like that, he actually saw me, and it was me he wanted.

"What are you doing after graduation?" he asked.

I had been wondering that for weeks, assuming I would never see him again. You have to know, he and I never spoke outside of our time together. We pretended we were classmates in passing. I resolved I would not ask him about his summer plans, which I hadn't.

"You mean the day of, or the summer?" I asked.

"The summer, dope," he said.

"Don't call me that," I said.

"I was joking," he said.

"Still," I said.

"Okay. Sorry," he said, kissing the top of my nose. He could be nice like that. "Silly?"

"I'm working part-time at the drugstore on Northern. Visiting family in Rhode Island and California."

“I want more of this,” he said, and took both my hands.

I shook my head. “You’re with Maria and I’m not into that.”

“Into what?” he said.

“Being your second girlfriend. Making out and all that—fine,” I said.

“Maria is Maria,” he said, sighing. “Let’s hang out once at least before the end of the summer.” I wanted to ask him if he was taking Maria to prom. “I’m not going to the prom. Maria and I broke up.”

Every time he said that, they would get back together.

“When I’m with you… there is something about you and I can’t stop coming back,” he said, kissing my neck this time. “How weird would it be that I love you?”

I thought about it for days after. If in these past two years he had grown to love me. It occurred to me that I didn’t know what love felt like.

*

Jen and Carol and I had disappeared into the bathroom for twenty minutes, trying on each other’s lipstick. I wasn’t going to look at them, Juan and Maria. I was going to pretend they didn’t exist, like I did in the hallways. But as I walked out of the bathroom, I almost hit the door in Maria’s face. I walked past her with my flock of friends, glad of the timing. And there he was. Juan. Standing outside the girls’ bathroom waiting for her. I breezed past him.

“Hey.”

I kept walking. Then gravity pivoted my body toward him, knowing Maria could walk out at any second. Jen turned around and saw us. She glared at me and stuck out her tongue sideways.

"What's up?" I asked.

"Nothing," he said, gave me a half-grin. "Just wanted to say hi."

I replayed this moment, not later than in the evening, before I passed out from all the beer swimming in my stomach, my tongue parched from too many cigarettes. It would be at the end of the summer when he would call me asking to hang out one more time before college classes started.

"Hi," I said.

"I didn't even recognize you at first," he said. He looked at my dress, my dark eyes.

"Well, it's me," I said.

Saying anything felt too easy and predictable, even for me. But I have drafted monologues since.

He didn't ask if I would be around later. But he was going to. I could tell from the way he was staring at me, like he did before we kissed. He could be the last boy, the only boy, who would ever want me. *Who would ever kiss me again?* is what I wondered. And then I thought of him and Maria in the backseat of the limo after prom.

I looked at his blue eyes one last time. I left. I heard him call my name and I kept walking.

After prom, me and the girls were on our way to Jimmy's Pub on MacDougal Street. Our great luck, the guy who drove the limo was a biker masquerading as a limo driver by night. He turned and looked at us, smiled in this cool-uncle fatherly way and said, "Private school kids, right?"

He let out a scraggly laugh and tossed a pack of Marlboro Reds, and it landed in my lap. We laughed.

“Alright,” he said. “We have two hours before you turn into pumpkins.”

As the limo raced down the Williamsburg Bridge, I lowered the window all the way and stuck out my full head like I’ve always wanted to do because it looked so cool in the movies. The air smelled warm and green, and the city lights were soon all around me. It felt like the first day of my life.

The driver pulled up in front of the pub. “Be back here in an hour or I’ll be coming in to get you,” he said.

We strode in and ordered Heinekens because we didn’t know any better, and played Nirvana songs on the jukebox. All six of us, beautiful and having no idea of it. Except for Carol.

I was all of myself, I thought, falling asleep that night. The beginning of me. And it was then that I made up my mind. At the end of the summer, I’d say no again.

"Dress to the nines
+ groove with ghosts..."
"dancing
with
myself"
"I feel so
extraordinary"
AKM25

PROM

Jared Harél

Mostly I remember those who went alone,
the unchosen who chose to dress to the nines
and groove with ghosts in a washed-out ballroom
while the rest of us paired up and posed
for stunned photos—stiff collars and pinned
corsages—then slow danced like rowboats
tied to a post. R hung with shadows and a proud
secret flask. L twist-and-shouted but didn't
smile once. I recall loud music. Oily skin.
How J got his ass dumped a couple days before
yet still wanted to ride in a limo. And that spurned
girl whose name I never learned—she turned
up in this scorching silver gown that tore
though us like starlight; rioted like a wound.

Jenny's Mixtape

Dodson Ng

"OK, so I will ask Maria, and you ask Jenny. Agreed?" Russell asked.

"Yeah... OK," David mumbled, but he was not sure.

His heart beat faster just thinking about asking Jenny to the prom. He looked at Russell. Russell must have sensed his nervousness. He had a big smile on his face and reassured David.

"Don't worry, it'll be fine. Maria will say yes, Jenny will say yes, and we'll all go together. It'll be great!" It wasn't fair. Of course, Maria would say yes. She and Russell were already dating, but David barely spoke to Jenny. Yes, he and Jenny had been in the same homeroom since they were freshmen, and technically, he did speak to her every day. (He took attendance, and she always answered "yes" when he called out her name. But did that really count?) But then there was also the mixtape incident, which he didn't want to think about now.

"... ah... yeah... but Sarge, I'm sure other guys will ask her..."

"But if you ask her first, she'll say yes."

"... I'm not sure about that logic..."

"You got this! Make sure you ask her soon. I gotta get to football practice."

Russell put David in a harmless headlock and exaggeratedly stamped his foot on the ground, making a loud noise, then grunted even louder as he released David. David laughed. Other kids barely glanced at them as they walked around them. Russell ran off.

*

David had known Russell since they were in junior high school. They sat next to each other and became fast friends, even though Russell was gregarious, and David was shy and quiet. They took turns hanging out at each other's houses after school most Friday afternoons. They read comic books and watched wrestling on TV together. Once, when they were at Russell's place, they cleared the center of the living room and pretended to wrestle. Russell was Sgt. Slaughter and David was Bob Backlund. They circled each other like the real wrestlers on TV. Then they both pounced!

Russell reached David first and tried to put him in the dreaded "Cobra Clutch." David eluded him and almost got him with the famous "Chicken Wing" maneuver, but then Russell lifted David up and body-slammed him onto the couch. But as David tried to escape, his foot hit the glass coffee table that had been moved aside. Clearly not enough. When they both realized what had happened, they stopped and stared at each other with bulging eyes. Upon inspection, the coffee table only sustained a small chip. It was barely noticeable. They moved all the pieces of furniture back to their normal positions before *WrestleMania* began and covered the coffee table with extra magazines.

Then they became quiet. Russell sat on the floor leaning against the couch. David sat on the couch. They had their comic books spread out between them. The room was quiet as a library until, inevitably, David burst out, "OMG, look what Magneto did to Wolverine!" David showed Russell the panels where an angry Magneto held Wolverine suspended in the air, with Wolverine gasping for breath. Russell stared at the pages, nodded, then turned back to his comic book.

A few minutes later, Russell looked over at David and said, "You're going to love the ending of *Daredevil*." David looked up and smiled, then went back to reading. Russell put down the issue of *Daredevil* and reached for the next comic book.

*

David walked to the subway and when he got on the N train headed to Queens, he put on his headphones and turned on his Walkman. All he could think about was Jenny. He didn't know why he adored her. Maybe it was because she was shy like him, and he knew she had a hidden beauty that just needed to be discovered, or maybe it was because she was really smart: he once unintentionally saw the "A" on her exam that he got a "B-" on. Or maybe it was her slim body, her cute smile, and the dot of a birthmark over the side of her mouth. It always looked like she had a dark crumb there. When he saw her up close, he had to hold himself back so as not to try to wipe it away. So, the question remained: how could he convince her to go to Senior Prom with him?

The music came through his headphones, New Order sang, *I feel so extraordinary, something's got a hold on me…* He just closed his eyes and began to bob his head. After a few moments, he opened his eyes abruptly and looked around; good, no one saw him. He turned off his Walkman and removed his headphones.

*

During the last few weeks of David's junior year, he discovered that he had become obsessed with Jenny. He thought of her in mundane moments: when he was brushing his teeth, when he was tying his shoelaces. He wanted to ask her out, but he just didn't know how. He asked Russell.

"So Sarge, what do you think I should do?"

"Just go up to her and ask her if she wants to go see a movie with you," Russell answered.

"But what if she wants to see a movie I don't want to see? Also, I don't have a car. How would we get there?"

"Look, you just take her to whatever movie she wants to go to."

"What about the car issue?"

"We can double date. I'll bring Maria. I'll try to borrow my mom's car, or maybe, since we're all in Queens, we can all just take the bus or subway to the Midway Theater."

David thought about this, but still had reservations. He procrastinated for days. Finals came and went, and he felt he missed the opportunity.

"You know it's really not too late to ask Jenny out," Russell offered.

"Yeah, but summer's here. I won't see her until the fall."

David felt the end of the semester was the end of seeing his "school friends." When summer arrived, he had to find a summer job. That was just the way it was.

"Maybe you can give her something so she won't forget about you over the summer. Do you know what she likes? Weren't you guys in any of the same classes?"

"Yeah, we were in History and Drafting together. Remember, I told you she started a conversation with me about Drafting."

"Yeah, she asked to borrow your eraser." Russell rolled his eyes.

"Yeah, but maybe she really wanted to talk to me and used that as an excuse?"

"Dude, maybe she left her eraser at home and needed to erase something and saw you had that huge white eraser sitting on your desk."

"How do you know I have the white eraser?"

"I used to sit next to you in junior high school. You used to take it out every morning right before class started and put it on the desk." They both laughed.

"OK, wait, do you think I should get her an eraser?!" David asked excitedly.

"No, you should not get her an eraser," Russell said in a deadpan tone. "Can you think of something else?"

"I can't get her a history book. That would be so lame… But I did overhear her talking to her friends once. I think she likes music."

"Great! You can get her a tape of something."

"But I don't know what music she likes."

"Just get her anything. It's a gift; everyone likes to receive gifts. Dude, don't overthink it."

David finally decided to give Jenny a mixtape—he would put a bunch of his favorite songs on it. She would really like that.

On the last day of school, without any preparation, with a trembling hand, in front of a group of her friends, he slid the mixtape across the desk to her. Her friends whispered to each other when he approached. Jenny looked at him, then looked at the cassette tape.

"… ah... I thought you might like this," David stammered.

"Oh… thank you," Jenny replied and gave him a gentle smile.

David walked briskly back to his desk to the sound of laughter and slouched in his chair, opened up a textbook, and pretended to read.

Later, he spoke to Russell.

"It was awful. I was so nervous. Her stupid friends were there laughing…"

"It's fine. She knows you made it for her, and she'll appreciate it. Don't worry about her dumb friends," Russell said and patted him on the back.

*

When David got off the subway and entered his house, he put his headphones back on and turned on his Walkman. Frankie Goes to Hollywood came on, telling everyone to *Relax, don't do it!* As he got some cookies from the shelf, his body just moved to the rhythm of the music. Erasure came next and begged, *Oh, baby, refrain from breaking my heart.* He continued to dance as he finished eating his cookies. When he finished, he sang, *Oh, baby, please, give a little respect to me.* When the song ended, he stopped singing; he stopped dancing, turned off his Walkman, and quietly put the dish in the sink. He went to the living room and started his homework.

After finishing, he came up with a plan. He would wait for the first moment that Jenny was alone and just ask her if she wanted to go to the prom with him. That would be nice and simple, no overthinking it.

The next day, David watched Jenny from afar, and finally, he saw her standing in front of the girls' bathroom. Alone. He took a deep breath and walked over to her.

"Hey Jenny," David said. She looked up and smiled at him. "Are you going to the prom with anyone?" But before he finished his question, he knew she would say no because he could see her smile turn. He saw the pity in her eyes. She began to slowly shake her head. He looked at her and nodded; the message was clear, and he understood; he walked away.

David found Russell before football practice and told him what happened.

"Hey dude, I'm sorry," Russell said.

"Yeah, thanks." David was devastated.

"I promise you, it'll be OK," Russell said as he put his hand on David's shoulder.

*

On the day of the prom, David found Russell between classes.

"Hey Sarge, I need you to do me a favor."

"Sure, what is it?"

"When you get to the prom, can you call me?"

"Are you sure you want me to do that? You know, you can go without a date. You can hang out with me and Maria. She likes you. It'll be good."

"No, I can't go like that. C'mon, you understand."

David didn't want to be a third wheel.

"So, call you when I get there. OK. Are you trying to figure out if Jenny will be there? I think it's OK to ask her."

"No, that's not it. Just give me a call when you get there. Oh, and what type of food do you think they'll serve at the prom?"

"OK, sure, I can give you a call when I get there. What food will they serve there? I don't know, I guess pizza, hot dogs, punch?" Russell gave David a puzzled look.

*

David was in his bedroom when the phone rang. He picked it up on the first ring.

"Hello?!" Russell asked.

"Yeah, I'm here," David answered.

"OK, it's kinda loud here!"

"Can you describe what's going on?"

"Sure, there are tables and chairs surrounding a big makeshift dance floor. Everyone is all dressed up. There are a couple of teachers by the food table, they're munching on hot dogs, and of course, there's punch and soda. They dimmed the lights. I don't see Jenny."

David could hear the music in the background: Billy Idol singing "White Wedding."

"It's OK, I'm not looking for Jenny. Thanks! Have a good night, Sarge!"

"I wish you were here, buddy!"

"Thanks," David replied and hung up the phone. He had moved his bed and desk and dresser against the bedroom walls. He had some microwaved bite-sized hot dogs and a can of soda on the desktop. He wore his dress pants and dress shirt, the same outfit he wore to many of his college interviews. He looked at the empty space in the middle of his bedroom. He put on his headphones. In his Walkman, he had a copy of the mixtape he made for Jenny. He fast-forwarded to one of his favorite songs. He dimmed the lights, but he didn't have to because now he closed his eyes, bobbed his head, swung his arms, and moved his feet as Billy Idol sang:

Oh, oh, dancing with myself
Oh, oh, dancing with myself
When there's nothing to lose, and there's nothing to prove
And I'm dancing with myself, oh, oh, uh-oh

'my whole heart...'

First Prom

Lisa Fitzsimmons Eddins

My Rose looks at her reflection in the mirror,
glitter in her hair, one set of lashes curled.
The most beautiful thing to come from me.

Her dress hangs on the door,
Size 7, ready to hug her hips.
Nothing like the plus, puffed sleeve drape I wore,
1980s rhinestones speckled over exaggerated curves.

Soon, a red-headed boy will arrive with corsage in hand.
Instead of a six-pack in the trunk.
They will dance, twirl under the twinkling lights,
his hand on her back.

He won't usher her to the door, to the beer, to the backseat.
She won't lower her eyes as she leaves the prom early.

My Rose flutters her finished lashes,
kisses her glossed lips in the mirror.
Smiles for herself and her perfect hair.

I help her dress, find her earrings, kiss her forehead.
The most beautiful thing to come from me.
I ask her to take a picture of the twinkling lights.
And we wait for the red-headed boy.

Can I Still Go to Prom? Mom?

Catherine Kanjer Kapphahn

"Can I still go to prom? Mom?" 18-year-old asks so innocently.

I blink. I'm silent. Didn't I just warn him the deadline for tickets was about to pass, didn't I pester him for weeks, didn't I say, why don't you just go with a group of friends? *Oh my God!* Is this going to be like senior pictures (when he almost missed the deadline) or senior sunrise (when he got the wrong morning) or senior sunset (when he got the wrong location) or the yearbook collage (when he almost didn't finish in time)?

"—Wait, what?—but you know the last day to buy prom tickets passed, right? Like, a while ago."

"I know, but you think I can still go?" he asks earnestly.

"Honestly, I don't know. You going with friends?" I say from behind the kitchen counter, as I wash dishes.

Teenage nod, "Yeah, people are going on their own, so… I'll meet people there."

"—Well, can you email the organizer and ask?" I encourage him as he shoves over the ever-growing pile of clean laundry on the couch. "*Like now*? Right now," I urge, again.

"Now?" He looks up, surprised. "Okay, I will. Why do we have all this laundry? There's no room for me to even sit."

"You're welcome to fold it," I say.

*

Last-minute tickets are available! $160.00 for dancing the night away under the glittering crystal chandeliers, and strolling to the outdoor terrace to admire the pinkish orange of the cinematic Queens skyline.

18-year-old loves music, he loves to dance, so I'm delighted he'll squeeze in this final high school rite of passage.

Between teaching my classes, I make clandestine calls and texts to moms with prom intel: Tux vs. Suit. Macy's sale vs. Men's Warehouse.

"We have to go now?" 18-year-old scowls. "I'm tired from school."

"—Yep, *now*, it's the only day I have to take you. I cannot do this without you." It's five days before prom.

"Okay, *okay*," he relents, then shrugs.

"You want to go to the city or Astoria?"

"Astoria," he says.

In 90-degree heat, we walk. Sweat beads gather on teenage forehead. Headphones are popped into ears. This year, I've been the most-hated parent, the one who drives him crazy, the one he's accused of being "frantic" countless times. He's been rejecting me high and low, and so, I'm absolutely *thrilled* to be walking with this guy anywhere!

Burlington Coat Factory, no luck. Local used clothing store: check! A brilliant peacock-blue, almost-new Kenneth Cole shirt for seven bucks. A group of teenage boys nearby tries on t-shirts between the racks, and sadness sweeps over me. Since the pandemic, 18-year-old has struggled to make close friends, a best friend, friends who visit him at our apartment. When will he find his pack? Still, I'm relieved he does have some friends at school.

On Steinway, we sit on a bench, sweating, waiting for the bus.

"It's so hot," he groans. His brown hair is disheveled and greasy; his bloodshot blue eyes look exhausted, yet he's also restless. In the past few months, he's been struggling to keep up in school. He seems burnt out. I pat his arm. He's been my whole world, and now we both have to make our own worlds.

A moment ago, I was carrying him as a newborn, and now, motherhood to children is over. What does it mean to be a mother to a young man? How do I learn to do that? I've been trying hard to step back and give him space. My own identity is shifting, and I wonder, where do I belong as a mother, a writer, and a teacher? What's my purpose now? Was I a good enough mom to 18-year-old?

At the Banana Republic Outlet, I bask in the air conditioning and hang out in the dressing room, running back and forth, bringing 18-year-old suits and jackets. Poor kid wore mostly hand-me-downs, and this, being in an actual store with him, is a rare occurrence. Since I'm here, I grab another room and try on dresses to wear to his graduation. When I emerge in a festive blue-red long dress, 18-year-old comes out in his latest suit and says, "Mom, that dress looks good!"

"Really?"

He nods and gives me an almost smile.

I'm shocked. Did he just say something nice? To me?

First real suit is bought. Belt, his dad orders online. Tie, I'll find from Pimbeche Vintage tomorrow. Black sneakers he already has, and that's the best we can do. Who wants to dance in new dress shoes anyway?

On the way home, he bursts out, the way many 18-year-olds often do, "I'm starving!" We pop into Djerdan Burek, a little Bosnian restaurant that reminds me of my Croatian mom and reminds 18-year-old of his only trip to his grandmother's country. Beef burek arrives, circular, flaky phyllo dough, filled with hot ground beef.

Across from each other, we sit quietly and eat. 18-year-old and I used to be close, used to talk easily about movies and his interests; he's a dreamer, an artist, an explorer, ever curious, and somehow he survived the pandemic a kind and empathetic teen. I was his supporter, his helper, until I helped too much, until I was more in relationship with his ADHD struggles than I was with him.

At 18, he suddenly became more critical, reactive, aloof, explosive, and distant. He began to separate and become his own human, as well he should. But no one tells you how much that's going to hurt. No one tells you how surprising that is. I recognize, as we eat in silence, that we've lost our closeness, and yet it feels as if right now, we're starting anew with this singular mission of a prom outfit.

*

The night of prom, 18-year-old concedes and I am permitted to take a few photos on the balcony. Against a brick wall, he poses proudly in his black suit with his brilliant blue shirt and vintage tie, and styled-back-with-gel brown hair.

Cologne wafts through the car as we drive him from Astoria to Terrace on the Park in Flushing Meadows, Corona Park. As my husband drives, we tell 18-year-old it was built for the World's Fair, and in 1965, The Beatles landed on the heliport there, and Madonna worked as an elevator attendant there (before she became Madonna).

18-year-old isn't impressed. He's half listening to us, half looking at his phone, until we pull up to the spaceship-like building on stilts.

"Is this it?" he asks with a nervous smile, leaning forward. Terrace on the Park is prom city tonight for several high schools. There are many excited, giddy teens in high heels, long and short, tightly fitted gowns, pressed tuxedos, suits of all colors, and polished black shoes. Nostalgic parents lean out windows or get out of their cars to snap photos.

Through our car's open window, 18-year-old suddenly hears someone call out his name. We pull over and say our goodbyes, tell him to be safe, to be careful.

"Okay, okay," he reassures us, forbidding us to take any more photos as he quickly slips out of the car. He shuts the door firmly, gives a quick wave. As he strides away, I watch from the rearview mirror. He greets some guys with bro-handshakes and then disappears into the crowd, into his very own prom night.

"sophisticated like satine..."
RAIN FOREST EXHIBIT
EVOLUTION AHEAD
NARS
AKA 25
"...in danger of becoming Beautiful..."

Friends Forever

Olena Jennings

I'm afraid to unravel in front of her
like the fragile velvet blouse
that comes apart at the seams.
From the same attic closet,
I find the plaid suit.
It is perfect for me to wear to the prom
at the Public Museum where we walk
through the streets of the past.

I envision my grandmother
in one of those houses, her hands
kneading dough as she tries to push
away the ominousness of late nights.
Later, the care needed in embroidery,
the needle pulling like my friend
pulls me down the ramps
of the rainforest section.

Time stands still
until we are in her bedroom, the night over.
Potpourri is poured out onto the floor
and she smells of patchouli. I hook the suit
on the door of the closet, which I don't go into
because I think I'll fall through. I am always
in danger of slipping away in her presence,
in danger of becoming beautiful.

Terre de Feu: Land of Fire

Ricki Richards

I felt pressured by time. I often waited until the last minute to do things, including buying a prom dress for a prom that wasn't my own. It was May 2009. Classes of my freshman year at New York University were wrapping up, and I was on the hunt for a prom dress to impress in the East Village. I chanced upon a small boutique on E 9th Street, called Meg. I was impressed by its simplicity. The curated, neutrally colored (i.e., mainly black) clothing was evenly spaced on bare-bones racks along the edges of the store and was looked over by a single salesperson—Meg herself. My eyes found it quickly… the perfect dress. Except it wasn't. It was four sizes too big and twice my budget. But it was perfect. It was three-quarter length instead of floor length, laced instead of beaded, matte instead of shiny. It wasn't like any other dress I had seen before at a prom. Its uniqueness appealed to me.

I played with the strapless dress in my hands, feeling the bumpy, yet delicate black lace over the tan underlining, mentally pairing it with black, strappy heels and light makeup. The mixture of desire and guilt at even the thought of spending money on this dress sat on my chest. But I had been working. I could spend my money on something other than tuition, right? The catalogue of dresses I borrowed from friends for dances when I was in high school sped through my mind. I went back and forth, not being able to make a decision, possibly to the annoyance of Meg. Spend the money, don't spend the money, spend the money, don't spend the money… She helped me pin the excess fabric so I could simulate the transformation from my usual uniform of a t-shirt and jeans to a state of elegance. Oh, and it would be extra for tailoring…

To my 19-year-old mind, this dress was a necessity. Nothing says "growing up" like buying a prom dress when you're broke and not in high school anymore.

My boyfriend at the time, Patrick, was a year younger than I, and he was now a senior at my alma mater, Mt. Carmel High School, in San Diego, California. Go Sundevils. We had started dating a year prior, when I was a senior and he was a junior. He was in a band that played once at a local coffee shop. I couldn't help myself. We were obsessed with each other. Some called it codependence. We called it love. I fell hard into the safety net of him, because the rest of my life hadn't been feeling very safe of late.

For our first prom together, he asked me to be his date by baking cookies in the shape of *Got PROM?* and had it sitting on the kitchen counter next to a glass of milk when I walked into his house after school. Just a few weeks before his cookie promposal and my impending high school graduation, I stood in his kitchen on the phone, my mom's jaw-clenched voice on the other end—a sure sign of her anger with me.

"Where are you?"

My heart raced, my mouth went dry. "I'm at Patrick's." (Duh.)

"I didn't know you were going there. You should be home. I don't like the way his mom treats his dad, anyways, it's not good for you to be around."

I think my mom resented their relationship because Patrick's parents seemed to actually *like* each other. My guess is that she also resented Patrick for taking me away from her, and she let me feel it.

I went straight to fix-it mode. "I'll come home right now."

"No, don't bother, Patrick is obviously more important to you anyways."

Back and forth we went, Patrick witnessing the one-sided conversation in silence, unsure how to handle me.

I begged her to let me make it better somehow, until I was on the floor of the kitchen, struggling for breath in the midst of a panic attack because I couldn't appease her. Come home and be with her or don't come home, both were wrong.

At this point, my parents were three years into a brutal divorce. My mom's pain made her particularly cruel toward my older sister and me—a symptom, I'm sure, of my dad's cruelty toward her. He struggled with alcoholism and was in a new relationship with his ex-best friend's ex-wife. My sister had been my shelter, but she ran away to college across the country early in our family's unraveling and left me alone to deal with the aftermath. A part of me felt abandoned, but I also couldn't wait to find my own place in the world like she was doing.

Growing up, our parents set money aside for college, and I "thanked them" by applying to only out-of-state schools, thereby guaranteeing I was going to be as far away from the mess of home as I could. I didn't have the wherewithal to be as grateful as I should have been until things went south, and it was at risk of being taken away. Somewhere in the middle of preparing for my Senior Prom and graduation—and committing to NYU (arguably one of the pricier joints around)—my dad decided he would no longer be sharing my full saved college fund with me; only a small percentage would go straight to the school. No other assistance would be provided. The divorce was too expensive.

I applied to as many scholarships as I could find, planned to get a job once I arrived in New York, and my mom insisted that no matter what, she would help me realize my dream of graduating from NYU at whatever cost, whatever loan. This was all on the heels of the financial crisis of 2008. My mom's job at a biomedical science startup had stopped paying her because they didn't have funding, but she stayed on for months, believing in their mission and their lie that "funding was coming." Money was tight, and it all felt impossible.

Prom Round One was a futile distraction. My friends and I went to the mall to get our makeup done at the MAC counter. Big mistake. Big. Huge. I sat there politely, watching them cake my face with product, not knowing how to tell them to *Stop! Please stop*. The makeup artist stepped back to look at their work. "Honey, you look great!" I walked out and went straight to the bathroom to scrape the layers of makeup off as best I could. I couldn't believe my friends talked me into spending money on this clownery. I lowered my t-shirt collar and saw the stark line where it went from orange MAC foundation at the base of my neck to my actual skin color.

The guilt I felt at spending the money, along with the devastation of not feeling pretty for my big Senior Prom night, wrecked my adolescent mind. Between my showy floor-length dress, the several inches of bra padding, and overdone makeup, I didn't feel like myself. The mood carried over into the evening. Despite prom being first and foremost a "dance," we didn't dance at all... except for about a minute of a slow dance. Classic.

With a year of college under my belt, I knew I would be able to approach Prom Round Two differently. I had a chance at a do-over. A chance to show just how cosmopolitan I had become in the Big City. I was going *back* to high school, even if it was just for one night.

Bellied up at Meg's checkout counter, I rode the wave of anxiety and relented, pulling out my hard-earned work-study job money to buy this perfect dress at this perfect East Village boutique. I would have to come back later to pick it up after the alterations were finished. How grown up! I found the strappy black heels (thank you, Union Square DSW) and set my mind on planning my own *simple* makeup. There would be no makeup counter at the mall this year, no way.

I marched to Sephora and bought myself a big girl brand of lipstick. *NARS Terre de Feu* red. A lipstick in another language? Get outta here. It was elevated, passionate, and delicate.

It meant "Land of Fire." It felt waxy and soft as I tamped it on, rarely gliding, to give it that sophisticated, feathered French look—light and effortless. Applying it made me feel like Satine from *Moulin Rouge*, Baz Luhrmann's fantastical 2001 musical romance starring Nicole Kidman as the courtesan who falls in love with a duke (who's actually a penniless writer), then dies of tuberculosis. Putting that lipstick on made me feel tragically romantic. It felt like a dream.

The thought of leaving New York and heading back to San Diego for the summer was bittersweet. Sure, I would get to show off this new dress, and my mature hair and makeup, but it also meant going back home to live with my mom for a couple of months. This brought about its own complications and heightened my feelings of neediness, tremendous love for her, and dread. To me, the dress was an embodiment of my breakaway, and I wasn't sure how this newfound confidence would translate to being back in her house. In avoidance, I put my full focus into prom... and Patrick.

Prom Round Two went off without a hitch. We had the limo, the friends, and the looks to go with a flawless evening. One of the best parts... I was able to go without a bra. This dress was fitted well enough that I didn't need one, thank you, custom tailoring. Patrick and I even danced most of the night. Looking back at pictures, I still don't really have a sense of whether I achieved the elegance I was going for, but buying that dress and lipstick was the first time I felt like I was stepping out on my own.

I still have the lipstick more than 16 years later. The nostalgia is too great to get rid of it. Yes, general wisdom says lipsticks should be thrown away after two years, but for those of you who are concerned it'll have me ending up like Satine... I assure you, it has yet to give me consumption. I still apply the lipstick for special occasions, like tonight. Each time I put on the *Terre de Feu* red, an appreciation for what it has endured with me surfaces, if even for a moment.

It's a connection to the portal of my previous life and what my mom and I withstood. Nowadays, my mom never fails to share how proud she is of me, specifically how proud she is of my bravery at moving across the country at such a young age all those years ago. Time helped us appreciate each other. We're getting closer to paying off those loans, too.

I wore the dress a few times after prom, relishing in the fact that it didn't look like a "prom dress." A couple of years ago, I gave it to one of my nieces, who is now nearly the age I was when I picked it out. I have no idea if she ever wore it to a dance, but I love knowing she has it.

Nothing says growing up like giving your prom dress to the next generation.

GOT PROM?

Acknowledgements

Thank YOU to everyone who made *Prom Queens* possible: The Astoria Bookshop, The World's Borough Bookshop, Queens Public Library, Queens Memory, Grove 34, Sunnyside Arts, New York Foundation for the Arts, Flushing Town Hall, Gabbing with Gays, Greater Astoria Historical Society, Frank Sinatra School of the Arts High School, and Palisades Convention Management, Inc.

Contributors

Pichchenda Bao is a Cambodian American poet and writer, infant survivor of the Khmer Rouge regime, daughter of refugees, and stay-at-home mother. Her most recent work has been published in *The Offing*, *SWWIM*, *Cultural Daily*, and elsewhere. She is co-editor of the poetry anthology, *Braving the Body* (Harbor Editions). She serves on the editorial board of QUEENSBOUND, an audio poetry project for Queens, NY, and has received fellowships and awards from Aspen Words, Kundiman, Bethany Arts Community, and Queens Council on the Arts. She lives, writes, and raises her three kids in New York City. More at pichchendabao.com.

Sydney Beveridge produces national radio talk shows on SiriusXM and has produced award-winning BBC radio documentaries and dramas with the Corporation for Independent Media. In late 2020, she and her husband also produced one baby (now a kid), who inspired her to create the "Progress Parenting" SiriusXM radio series. She also produces a daily "Mom Haiku" that she posts on social media, for now. She can be found tapping a toe in the produce aisles of her local Astoria grocery stores.

Lisa Fitzsimmons Eddins is an English professor, trainer, instructional systems designer, writer, and mother of five who resides in Northeast Florida with her husband and youngest daughter, Rose. While she is more of a technical writer than a creative, she aspires to write more poetry. When not working, Lisa enjoys traveling, day trips to Disney World, and restoring vintage toys and dolls (visit missrosiesdolls.com to learn more). Lisa loves visiting her sister in Queens, and on a recent trip, she had the privilege of attending a writing workshop at Sunnyside Arts, which inspired her to craft the poem in this anthology.

Ari Figueroa is a writer in their 30s living in Astoria, Queens. Originally from Massachusetts, they've been writing since they were seven and never stopped. Plays, short stories, poetry, and piles of journals fill Ari's written word repertoire. Ari is also a teacher, DnD DM, drag queen, trivia host, and more! This is Ari's first published poem, dedicated to their Nana.

Kelly Jean Fitzsimmons is a Queens-based writer, college essay writing instructor, and storyteller. Her nonfiction work has appeared in *HiLoBrow*, *Marie Claire*, *Hippocampus Magazine*, and numerous anthologies. She is the creator and producer of No, YOU Tell It! (noyoutellit.com), a nonfiction series that brings storytellers together to trade tales, speak each other's words, and empower voices on the page and stage. Kelly Jean is also the editor of the *No, YOU Tell It! Ten-Year Anthology*, available from Palm Circle Press. Visit kellyjeanfitzsimmons.com and follow @kjfitzsimmons for more.

Jane Frances (she/they) is from Queens, NY, and won't ever let you forget it. By day, she teaches English to the youth of the city, and by night, she enjoys what her hometown has to offer.

Lakshmi Gandhi is a writer, journalist, and editor who lives in Jackson Heights, Queens. A proud alum of the No, YOU Tell It! storytelling series, she has focused on telling stories about Asian American identity throughout her career. Her work has appeared in NBCNews.com, NPR's Code Switch blog, HISTORY.com, and *The Washington Post*, among many other publications. She is a graduate of CUNY's Newmark School of Journalism and Bryn Mawr College.

Jared Harél's most recent poetry collection, *Let Our Bodies Change the Subject* (University of Nebraska Press, 2023), won the Prairie Schooner Raz-Shumaker Book Prize and was named a finalist for the Paterson Poetry Prize and the National Jewish Book Award. Awarded the Stanley Kunitz Memorial Prize from *American Poetry Review* as well as the William Matthews Prize from *Asheville Poetry Review*, Jared is an editorial board member and co-curator for QUEENSBOUND—a collaborative Queens audio project founded by KC Trommer. For more information, visit: jaredharel.com.

Abeer Y. Hoque is a Nigerian-born Bangladeshi American writer and photographer. She likes dressing up, old trees, and velveteen. Her books include a coffee table book (*The Long Way Home*), a linked collection of stories, poems, and photographs (*The Lovers and the Leavers*), and a memoir (*Olive Witch*). See more at olivewitch.com.

Vegas K Jarrow is the rebirth of Vijay R. Nathan, who is the pen name of Vijay Ramanathan. This particular stream of human consciousness grew up in Staten Island, New York City. He is a two-time Master's degree-earning poet. His published books include *Escape from Samsara*, *Celebrity Sadhana*, and *Breakdown Dancer*, the last published by Poets of Queens Press. He worked for 15 years with Queens Public Library and appreciates the diverse flavors of all the neighborhoods in Queens. Go to his linktree, handle Vegas Jarrow, to explore the rabbit holes that represent what he has become.

Olena Jennings is the author of the poetry collection *The Age of Secrets* (Lost Horse Press), the chapbook *Memory Project*, and the novel *Temporary Shelter* (Cervena Barva Press). She is the translator or co-translator of collections by Ukrainian poets Kateryna Kalytko (co-translated with Oksana Lutsyshyna), Iryna Shuvalova, Vasyl Makhno, and Yuliya Musakovska. Her translation of Anna Malihon's *Girl with a Bullet* was released in October 2025 from World Poetry Books. She lives in Queens, New York, where she founded and co-curates the Poets of Queens reading series and press.

Catherine Kanjer Kapphahn is a writer, educator, and storyteller. Her memoir *Immigrant Daughter: Stories You Never Told Me* received The Center for Fiction's Christopher Doheny Award and was published by Audible. Catherine received grants from Queens Council on the Arts and City Artist Corps. Her writing has appeared in QUEENSBOUND, *Motherwell Magazine*, *The Handbook of Disability-Affirmative Systemic Therapy*, *Croatia Week*, *Newtown Literary*, and the Feminist Press Anthology *This is the Way We Say Goodbye*. Catherine is an adjunct lecturer at City University of New York at Lehman College in the Bronx and a yoga teacher in Queens.

Ashley King, also known as **A King McCarty**, is a multidisciplinary storyteller based in Astoria, Queens. She is a visual artist, actor, musician, writer, composer, and theatrical producer. Her works have been seen on stages and gallery walls throughout NYC and the United States, including in Queens at Grove 34, QED, Culture Lab, The Factory, and at numerous community events near Astoria Park/

Ditmars. She is an enthusiastic supporter of local artists and created *Artstoria New York* to share news of the arts in her neighborhood and create new works inspired by her community. Frequent collaborators include No, YOU, Tell It!, Astoria Park Alliance, Destination Ditmars, and Long Island City Artists.

Mary Lannon's unpublished novel, *Tide Girl*, was a finalist for the 2023 PEN\Bellwether Prize for Socially Engaged Fiction. Her stories have appeared at *Necessary Fiction*, *Story*, *New World Writing*, and elsewhere. She teaches writing and women and gender studies at Nassau Community College in Long Island, NY, and lives in Kew Gardens, where she runs a reading series at the local cemetery. More information at MaryLannon.com.

Tim Lindner is a writer and project manager who has been working with No, YOU Tell It! as a story coach and co-producer since 2020. Tim has published poems in *The Northern Virginia Review*, *Awakenings Review*, *Artemis Journal*, and other notable publications. He is also the editor of *The Book of Life After Death*, a collection of stories and poems about death and grieving, published by Tolsun Books in September 2023.

Dodson Ng is a writer based in Queens, NY. His short story, "Ok," was published in *Newtown Literary*, and "Thoo-por" was published in *Asian Voices*.

Ricki Richards made her life debut in California and moved to New York to obtain a nursing degree at NYU. Professionally steeped in soapy water, her career has been dedicated to teaching young minds the murky art of hand-washing through her service as a Youth Public Health Educator in the Peace Corps and many years as a School Nurse in New York City. She is the co-creator and co-Race Director of the Queens-based "Bridge and a Slice Half Marathon" and "Hot Dog Eater 50 Kilometer" races and has completed multiple ultra-marathon distances. A believer in the healing power of stories and storytelling, Ricki built and maintains a free community "Mosaic Your Mind" mini library, and as an amateur documentarian, is in the process of making a documentary about running entitled "Bruised Toes."

Zach Rothman-Hicks is an educator and multimedia conceptual artist who creates intergenerational LGBTQIA+ performances and oral history projects. He is the creator and producer of *Gabbing with Gays*, an interactive, multidisciplinary community arts project initiated in 2021, whose aim is to explore and refine tools that enable profound connections through the creation of a shared liminal space. Follow @gabbing_with_gays for more.

Anda Totoreanu is an immigrant, poet, immigration lawyer, choral singer, and lover of all things outdoors. Her poems have been published by *The Poetry Society of New York*, *Pandemic Poems*, *Gravel Literary Journal*, and *Poets of Queens*. She has also published work in several academic journals for her research on minority rights and conflict resolution. Anda's poetry explores themes of (self) love, loss, vulnerability, family, identity, coming to terms with the past, living in the present, and the peace of finding oneself in nature. You can find many of her poems at instagram.com/poemsbyanda/. She received her creative writing minor from Lafayette College.

KC Trommer (she/her) is the author of *We Call Them Beautiful* (Diode Editions, 2019) and *The Hasp Tongue* (dgp, 2014). In 2018, she founded QUEENSBOUND, an ongoing public poetry series on the 7 train. She holds a BA in English from the University of Georgia and an MFA in Poetry from the University of Michigan Helen Zell Writers' Program. She lives in Jackson Heights, Queens, with her son.

Aida Zilelian is a first-generation American-Armenian writer, educator, and storyteller. She is the author of novels *The Legacy of Lost Things*, *All The Ways We Lied*, and debut poetry chapbook *Dissonance*, winner of the Swan Scythe's chapbook contest. She has told stories across the country, in Los Angeles, Montreal, and most recently, televised on PBS' Stories from the Stage. She recently completed her full-length poetry collection, *Beautiful Monster* (and other lost orphans). This year, she will be giving her first TEDx talk, scheduled for April 2026 in the Dominican Republic.